Grade Boosters

BOOSTING YOUR WAY TO SUCCESS IN SCHOOL

Second Grade Language Arts, Reading, and Math

SUPER EDITION

By Vicky Shiotsu, Faybeth Harter,
Susan Williams, and Zondra Knapp

Illustrated by Eve Guianan and Lucy Helle

LOWELL HOUSE JUVENILE

LOS ANGELES

NTC/Contemporary Publishing Group

Published by Lowell House
A division of NTC/Contemporary Publishing Group, Inc.
4255 West Touhy Avenue, Lincolnwood (Chicago), Illinois 60646-1975 U.S.A.

Lowell House books can be purchased at special discounts
when ordered in bulk for premiums and special sales.
Contact Customer Service at the above address,
or call 1-800-323-4900.

Printed and bound in the United States of America

ISBN: 0-7373-0151-1

10 9 8 7 6 5 4 3 2 1

Contents

BOOSTING SUCCESS IN SCHOOL

Grade Boosters: Second Grade Language Arts, Reading, and Math presents activities that let your child experience learning in a stimulating and enjoyable way. These age- and grade-appropriate activities help boost self-esteem.

How to Use This Book

Grade Boosters: Second Grade Language Arts, Reading, and Math offers your child a variety of activities that will enhance his or her understanding of each subject. These activities help youngsters acquire fundamental skills while using critical and creative thinking. In particular, the clever puzzles and games activities encourage your child to explore concepts in a unique and entertaining way.

As your child works through the pages, give praise and encouragement. Each activity is designed to ensure success and stimulate interest. If your child likes to work independently, let him or her do so. If your child prefers to read aloud, then by all means do that.

There are review pages throughout each section, which check your child's progress on mastering the skills taught in that section. Achievement awards help develop your child's sense of accomplishment and academic success. Encourage your child to cut out these awards and put them in a special place where your family can recognize your child's accomplishments.

Two important features also appear throughout the book. TOGETHER TIME, designed especially for interactive learning, offers activities for you and your child to do together. The GRADE BOOSTER! feature specifically promotes critical and creative thinking skills. These are precisely the skills that will become vital to your child's future academic success—and success in life.

Note to Parents

Time Spent Together

The time you spend with your child as he or she learns is invaluable. Therefore, the more positive and constructive the environment you can create, the better. In working together, allow your child the freedom to go at his or her own pace. If your child would like to talk about the pictures, all the better. Allow your child to freely share and express opinions. Ask questions about what your child sees. Encourage your child to predict actions or events, or even make up a story about what he or she sees on the page. Be creative!

Remember to consider your child's ability. Because the activities range from easy to more difficult, you may need to work with your child on some of the pages. Read the directions and explain them. Go over the examples that are given. While creativity should be encouraged and praised, help your child look for the best answer. The answer key in the back of the book will help you guide your child.

Work together only as long as he or she remains interested. If necessary, practice only a few pages at a time. Before going on to a new page, always review work just completed. This will ensure better recall. The exercises should be done consecutively within each section, as the activities on each page build on the skills presented on the pages that precede it. Your child may want to skip from section to section, covering a little bit of math and reading in one day. Encourage your child to explore his or her interests. Remember that eagerness, willingness, and success are much more important in the long run than exactness and perfection. Remember, too, that your child's level of participation will vary at different times. Sometimes a response may be brief and simplistic; at other times, a response may be elaborate and creative. Allow room for both. Much more learning will take place in a secure, accepting environment.

Positive experiences promote positive attitudes, including a desire to learn and a curiosity about the world. You can be an instrumental tool in helping your child develop a positive attitude toward learning. Your "one-on-one" contact cannot be duplicated at school. Therefore, you have a choice opportunity to share with your child as he or she learns about the world around us.

THIS BOOK BELONGS TO . . . ME!

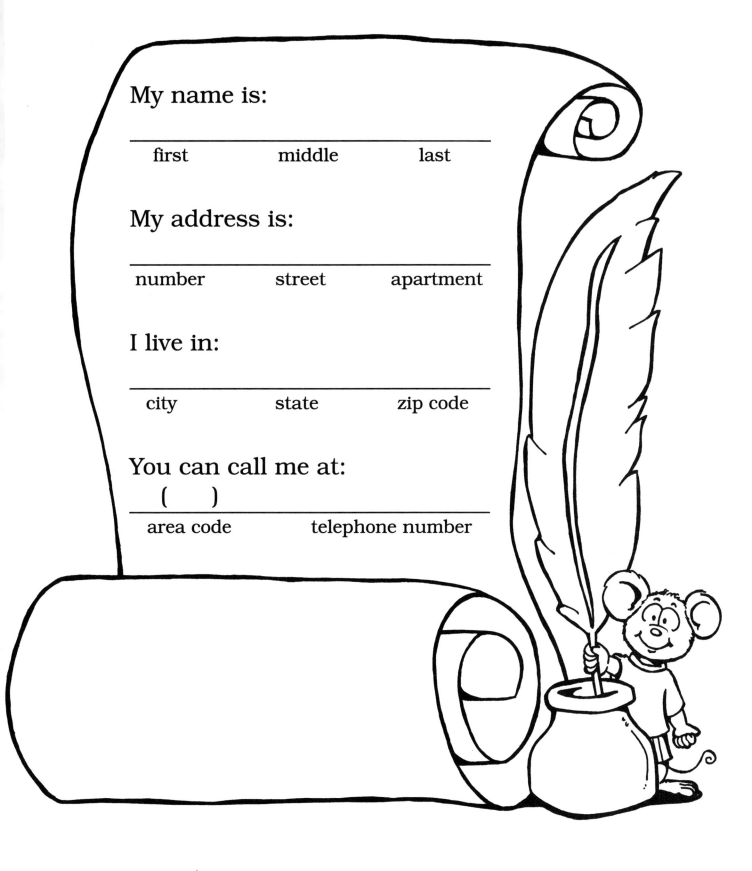

My name is:

_____
first   middle   last

My address is:

_____
number   street   apartment

I live in:

_____
city   state   zip code

You can call me at:
( )
_____
area code   telephone number

Language Arts

This section is designed to give children an opportunity to practice their basic language skills. Children will become familiar with capitals, punctuation, plurals, contractions, synonyms, antonyms, and homonyms. Activities include identifying complete and incomplete sentences, rearranging word order, alphabetizing, and creative writing. This section also focuses on improving and developing vocabulary.

I know my letters
and sounds.

Now I am going
to practice using
words and sentences!

FREDDY'S STORY

Freddy Frog has written a story. Look carefully. Can you see what he has forgotten to do?

> my friend is coming today. we are going to play tag. then we are going to catch flies. it will be fun!

Freddy forgot that every sentence begins with a capital letter. Can you help him? Circle the letters that need to be capitals. Then rewrite the story correctly on the lines.

_____

_____

_____

_____

_____

GRADE BOOSTER!

On another sheet of paper, write a story telling what you like to do with your friends for fun. Remember to use a capital letter at the beginning of each sentence!

Skills: using capital letters, writing sentences

NAMES AROUND THE WORLD

The names of people and places begin with capital letters. Read the sentences below. Circle the names that need capitals. Write the names correctly on the lines.

My name is peter. I'm from russia.

My name is keiko. I'm from japan.

_____

_____

My name is ingrid. I'm from sweden.

My name is jomo. I'm from kenya.

_____

_____

My name is duncan. I'm from scotland.

My name is maria. I'm from mexico.

_____

_____

Write a sentence that tells your name and where you are from. _____

_____

A MAP OF ANYTOWN

The map below shows that names of certain places in a community begin with capital letters. Answer the questions about Anytown. Don't forget capital letters!

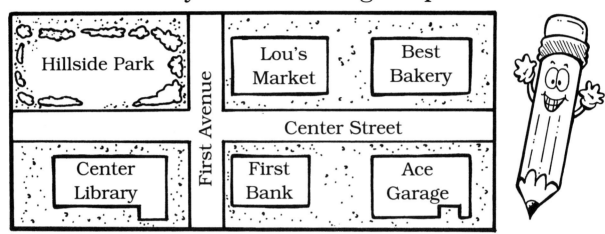

1. What is the name of the park? _____

2. On what street is the bakery? _____

3. Where could you buy soup? _____

4. What is the name of the library? _____

5. What is the name of the bank? _____

6. Where could you fix your car? _____

7. Which store sells birthday cakes? _____

TOGETHER TIME: Ask an adult to help you look in the Yellow Pages. Write a name for each of these places in your community:

restaurant _____

bookstore _____

Skills: capitalizing the names of particular places, reading a map

ALL THROUGH THE YEAR

The names of the days and months begin with capital letters.

Sunday	January	July
Monday	February	August
Tuesday	March	September
Wednesday	April	October
Thursday	May	November
Friday	June	December
Saturday		

Answer the questions. Don't forget to use capitals!

1. What day is today? _____

2. What day will tomorrow be? _____

3. What day was yesterday? _____

4. What month is it? _____

5. What will next month be? _____

6. In what month is your birthday? _____

7. In what month does school end? _____

8. What is your favorite month? _____

Skills: identifying the names of days and months, using capital letters

TERRIFIC TITLES

The first word of a title always begins with a capital letter. Important words in the title also begin with capital letters.

Example: **T**he **C**at in the **H**at

Write the book titles correctly on the lines.

fun in space ①	all about dogs ②	a surprise at school ③	real heroes ④	looking at trees ⑤

1. _____

2. _____

3. _____

4. _____

5. _____

Suppose you were going to write a book about yourself. Write its title on the book, then decorate the cover.

Skill: capitalizing the words in book titles

DINOSAUR DAYS

A sentence that **tells** something ends with a **period**.

A sentence that **asks** something ends with a **question mark**.

Examples: Most dinosaurs were huge.

Did dinosaurs swim**?**

Read the sentences below. Put a period or a question mark at the end of each sentence.

1. Dinosaurs lived millions of years ago

2. How big were the largest dinosaurs

3. Which dinosaur was the smallest

4. Some dinosaurs had horns

5. Dinosaurs hatched from eggs

6. Many dinosaurs ate plants

7. Did all dinosaurs have tails

8. Why did the dinosaurs die out

TOGETHER TIME: Ask an adult to help you find the answers to at least two of the questions above.

A SEA OF SENTENCES

Sentences that show strong feeling end with an **exclamation mark**.

Example: Wow! Look at that dolphin!

Read the sentences. Put a period, a question mark, or an exclamation mark at the end of each sentence.

1. It is peaceful in the water

2. Do you like to swim in the sea

3. Watch out for that shark

4. Is that an octopus

5. Get out of the way

6. Many animals live in the sea

7. Look at the size of that whale

8. Do all sea animals have scales

GRADE BOOSTER!

On a separate sheet of paper, write three sentences about the sea. Use a period, a question mark, and an exclamation mark.

Skills: using end punctuation, comprehension

ABBREVIATIONS SEARCH

An **abbreviation** is a group of letters that stands for a longer word. Many abbreviations begin with a capital letter and end with a period.

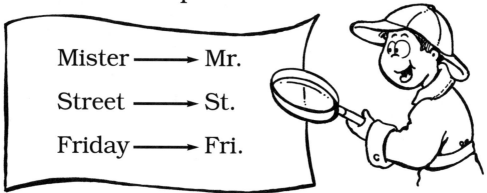

Mister ⟶ Mr.

Street ⟶ St.

Friday ⟶ Fri.

An abbreviation is hiding in each sentence below. Circle the abbreviations and write them correctly on the lines.

1. Kelly's birthday is nov 21. _____

2. Give this book to mrs Carlson. _____

3. The party will be on apr 11. _____

4. My doctor's name is dr Brown. _____

5. Sandy was born on feb 4, 1991. _____

6. We saw mr Lee at the mall. _____

7. School starts on sept 8. _____

Write your address below. Circle the abbreviations.

_____

_____

A SPECIAL PET

Rewrite the sentences. Use capital letters. Put in periods, question marks, and exclamation marks.

Write a sentence about a pet you would like to own. End your sentence with a period, a question mark, or an exclamation mark. Don't forget to use capital letters!

_____

_____

Skills: demonstrating mastery of capital letters and punctuation

COOL KID AWARD

presented to

_____
(my name)

for SUPER-COOL work with capital letters and punctuation!

CLOWN AROUND WITH PLURALS

Plurals are words that mean more than one. Add **s** or **es** to the words on the balloons to make plurals.

circus___ glass___ clown___ box___ tent___ whistle___ dish___ bunch___ cage___ sandwich___ bush___ wagon___

Add **s** to most words.

Add **es** to words that end in **s, x, sh,** or **ch**.

TOGETHER TIME: Ask someone at home to give you a spelling test with the above plurals. See how many words you can spell on your own!

Skills: writing plurals that end in **s** and **es**

UP, UP, AND AWAY!

Write the plural of each word on the hot-air balloon.

If a vowel comes before the **y,** just add **s.**

boy – boys

If a consonant comes before the **y,** change the **y** to **i** and add **es.**

sky – skies

story _____   day _____

buggy _____   city _____

tray _____   penny _____

key _____   berry _____

pony _____   monkey _____

hobby _____   family _____

valley _____   donkey _____

Skills: understanding and writing plural forms of words that end in **y**

TRICKY PLURALS

Some words have the same form for both singular and plural meanings. Other words change forms completely.

Write the plural of each word. Use the words on the hat.

one **deer** – two **deer**

one **mouse** – two **mice**

man _____

sheep _____

fish _____

ox _____

foot _____

woman _____

tooth _____

goose _____

child _____

moose _____

oxen	feet
teeth	men
fish	sheep
geese	women
moose	children

GRADE BOOSTER!

Write a sentence using at least three tricky plurals.

_____

_____

Skills: understanding and writing irregular plurals

FUN WITH PLURALS

Write the plural of each word.

1. brush __ __ __ __ __ ⃝ __

2. bus __ ⃝ __ __ __

3. toy ⃝ __ __ __

4. apple __ __ __ ⃝ __ __

5. fox ⃝ __ __ __ __

6. dress __ ⃝ __ __ __ __ __

7. man __ ⃝ __

8. family __ __ __ __ __ ⃝ __ __

9. tooth __ __ __ ⃝ __

10. sheep ⃝ __ __ __ __

11. bench ⃝ __ __ __ __ __

Riddle Time! Which insects like toast?

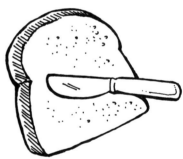

To find the answer, write each circled letter over the matching numbered line.

__ __ __ __ __ __ __ __ __ __ __
11 2 3 9 7 6 5 4 8 1 10

SAIL WITH CONTRACTIONS

Contractions are words that are made from two words with one or more letters left out. The missing letters are replaced by an **apostrophe** (').

Write the contraction for each pair of words.

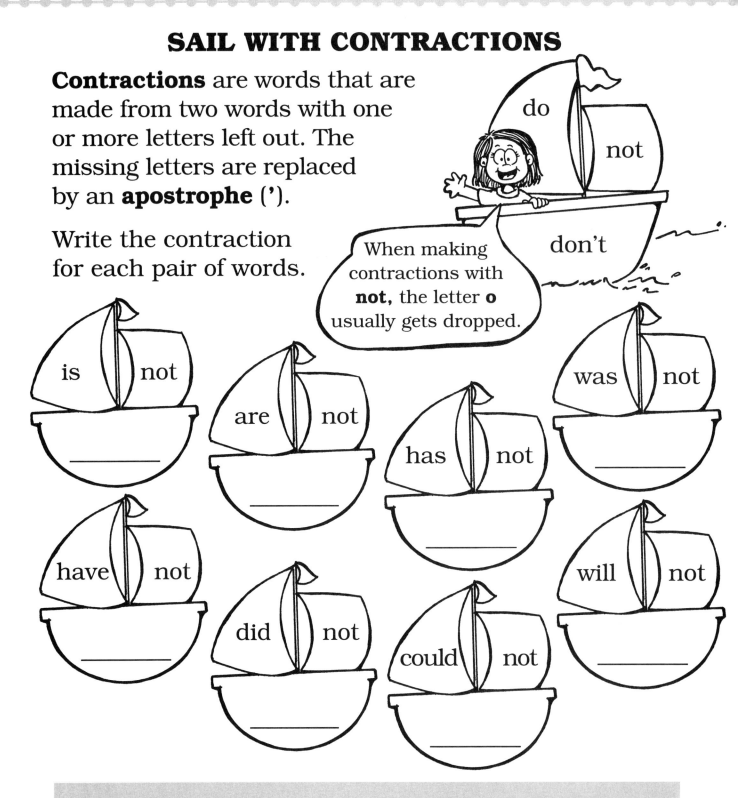

When making contractions with **not,** the letter **o** usually gets dropped.

do
not
don't

is | not

are | not

has | not

was | not

have | not

did | not

could | not

will | not

TOGETHER TIME: Do this activity with someone at home. Take turns completing these three sentences: *Yesterday I didn't . . . I don't like to . . . I won't ever . . .*

Skills: recognizing and writing contractions

JEFF'S LETTER

Help Jeff finish his letter on the computer by writing the correct contraction on each line. Use words from the box. Use each word only once.

she's	they're
he's	We're
It's	you're
	I'm

Hi, Grandpa!

_____ going to be fun visiting you at your cabin. Mom said _____ going to write you a letter today. Mom and Dad are so busy that _____ both happy to go on vacation. Dad said _____ going to take me fishing with him. _____ so excited I can't sleep! I hope _____ excited about seeing us, too! _____ all looking forward to the trip. See you soon!

Love,

Jeff

ON THE MOVE

Write the contraction for the
two words below each line.

Drop the letters
w and **i** for
contractions
with **will**.

1. ___*I'll*___ ride my bike.
   I will

2. _____ go to school by bus.
   He will

Drop the letters
h and **a** for
contractions
with **have**.

3. _____ gone to the airport.
   They have

4. _____ have fun on the plane.
   You will

5. _____ been on a truck before.
   We have

6. Lynn said _____ go rowing.
   she will

7. _____ bought a ticket for the ferry.
   I have

8. Tom said _____ travel by train.
   he will

GRADE BOOSTER!

Write a sentence using at least two contractions.

_____

_____

_____

Skills: understanding and writing contractions

TREETOP CONTRACTIONS

Follow the directions on the tree trunks.

do not _____

is not _____

it is _____

he is _____

she will _____

you are _____

they have _____

will not _____

I'm _____

she's _____

we're _____

aren't _____

hasn't _____

they're _____

we'll _____

couldn't _____

Write the contraction for each pair of words.

Write the two words that make up each contraction.

Skills: reading and writing contractions

29

THE NAME GAME

Write each group of names in alphabetical order.

Amy **B**rad **C**arl **D**ana

Look at the first letter of each word for help.

Meg
Kyle
Jodi
Pam

1. _____
2. _____
3. _____
4. _____

Evan
Rob
Sue
Hans

1. _____
2. _____
3. _____
4. _____

Teri
Will
Greg
Bob

1. _____
2. _____
3. _____
4. _____

Fred
Val
Ned
Lynn

1. _____
2. _____
3. _____
4. _____

GRADE BOOSTER!

Choose four people you know. Write their names in alphabetical order.

1. _____   3. _____
2. _____   4. _____

Skill: alphabetizing words according to the first letter

BUSY BEES

Write the words on the flowers in alphabetical order. Look at the **second** letter of each word for help.

bee
bold
bright
buzz

hive
happy
hurry
honey

1. _____
2. _____
3. _____
4. _____

flower
food
fresh
field

1. _____
2. _____
3. _____
4. _____

sticky
syrup
sweet
smooth

1. _____
2. _____
3. _____
4. _____

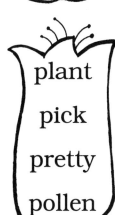

plant
pick
pretty
pollen

1. _____
2. _____
3. _____
4. _____

TOGETHER TIME: Play this game with a partner. Get 16 slips of paper and write a word on each one. Put the papers in a lunch bag. Take turns shaking the bag, drawing four words, and arranging them in alphabetical order. Put the papers back into the bag after each turn.

Skill: alphabetizing words according to the second letter

AT THE ZOO

Unscramble the sentences by writing the words in alphabetical order. Don't forget capital letters and periods!

1. lion   roared   big   a

A big lion roared.

2. munched   four   quietly   giraffes

_____

3. on   bear   a   rocks   climbed

_____

4. saw   people   several   snakes

_____

5. fed   a   squirrels   child   some

_____

6. trunks   their   elephants   raised

_____

7. of   swam   group   a   seals

_____

Skill: alphabetizing words according to the first and second letters

(my name)

did a s-s-splendid job learning basic word skills!

MAKE NEW WORDS

A **prefix** is one or more letters added to the beginning of a word. A prefix changes the meaning of a word. For example, the prefixes **un** and **dis** mean "not." A person who is **unselfish** is not selfish. A person who **disagrees** does not agree.

Add **un** to these words and rewrite them.

happy _____   lock _____   tie _____

Add **dis** to these words and rewrite them.

obey _____   like _____   honest _____

Complete the sentences with the words you wrote.

1. The child was _____ when he lost his dog.

2. I will _____ the knot for you.

3. People who lie are _____.

4. Dad must _____ the door to get inside.

5. It is wrong to _____ the law.

6. I _____ peas and carrots.

Write a sentence using both **unlucky** and **disappear**.

_____

_____

Skills: adding prefixes to words, using context clues

LET'S DO IT AGAIN!

A prefix is added to the beginning of a word. The prefix **re** means "again." For example, if you **rewrite** a story, you write it again.

rewrite	rewrap
repaint	reheat
rebuild	replant
reread	repack

Use the words on the paper to complete the sentences.

1. Jan will _____ the buns in the oven.

2. Dad is going to _____ the house blue.

3. Max will _____ the tower of blocks that fell.

4. I will _____ the gift because the paper tore.

5. Mom has to _____ the tulip bulbs.

6. Let's _____ the note on a new sheet of paper.

7. We will _____ the suitcase because it's too full.

8. I like this book so much I'm going to _____ it at least one more time.

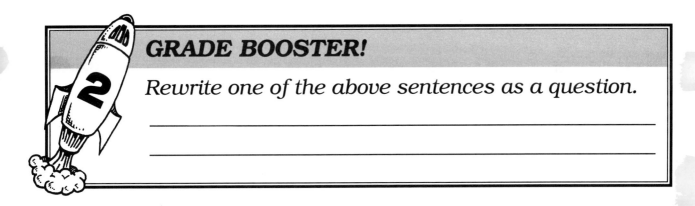

GRADE BOOSTER!

Rewrite one of the above sentences as a question.

_____

_____

SWINGING WITH SUFFIXES

Suffixes are one or more letters added to the end of a word. The suffix **ful** means "full of." The suffix **less** means "without." For example, someone who is **careful** does things with care. Someone who is **careless** does not take enough care.

Fill in the blanks. Add **ful** or **less** to the word at the end of each sentence.

1. Something that hurts is _____. (pain)

2. Something that does not hurt is _____. (pain)

3. Items that serve a good purpose are _____. (use)

4. Items that have no use are _____. (use)

5. A person who is brave is _____. (fear)

6. A person who is scared is _____. (fear)

7. Something that has no color is _____. (color)

8. Something that is full of color is _____. (color)

9. A person who helps another is _____. (help)

10. A person who cannot look after himself or herself is _____. (help)

Skills: writing words with suffixes, comprehension

A SPECIAL DAY

The suffix **ly** means "in the manner of." Words that end in **ly** usually describe actions.

Read the story. Circle the words that end in **ly**. Write each word beside its meaning on the lines below.

The sun shone brightly through Lisa's bedroom window. Lisa opened her eyes slowly. Suddenly, she jumped out of bed. She ran to the kitchen and then squealed happily. Her parents were sitting quietly around the table in front of a colorful cake. When they saw Lisa, they called out loudly, "Happy Birthday!"

1. moving without much speed _____

2. with joy _____

3. giving much light _____

4. in a noisy way _____

5. fast or without warning _____

6. making little or no noise _____

GRADE BOOSTER!

Write three more words that end in **ly**.

_____ _____ _____

WORDY BIRDS

Look at the words on the birds.
Color the birds:

• red if the word has only a prefix

• blue if the word has only a suffix

• yellow if the word has both a prefix and a suffix

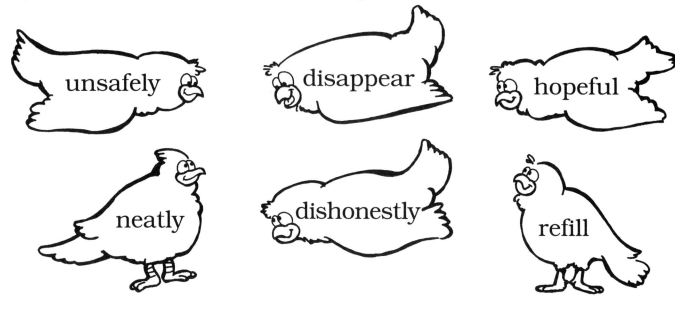

unsafely
disappear
hopeful
neatly
dishonestly
refill

Use the words on the birds to complete the sentences.

1. Don't ride your bike _____.

2. Jim is _____ that he will win the prize.

3. Karen writes very _____.

4. The magician made a bird _____ in a box.

5. I need to _____ the water bottle.

6. He acted _____ when he stole the money.

SPORTY SYNONYMS

Synonyms are words that have the same, or almost the same, meaning. For example, **fast** and **quick** are synonyms.

Look at each row of words. Underline the two words that are synonyms.

1. throw   toss   catch
2. jump   swim   leap
3. sing   shout   cheer
4. weak   strong   mighty
5. prize   team   award
6. boring   exciting   thrilling

The pairs of synonyms above are hidden in the puzzle. Circle each word. The words go down or across.

a	s	t	r	o	n	g	l	e	r	m	t	o	s	t
w	h	l	e	a	s	x	e	r	w	i	h	e	t	h
a	o	a	j	u	m	p	a	z	u	g	r	x	r	r
r	u	w	p	r	i	v	p	s	h	h	e	c	o	o
d	t	o	s	s	b	e	x	c	i	t	i	n	g	w
s	t	r	v	p	r	i	z	e	a	y	j	u	t	h
c	h	e	e	r	x	t	h	r	i	l	l	i	n	g

READ UP ON ANTONYMS

Antonyms are words that have opposite meanings. For example, **long** and **short** are antonyms.

little	never	back
end	new	full
over	weak	quiet

Write the words from the box beside their antonyms.

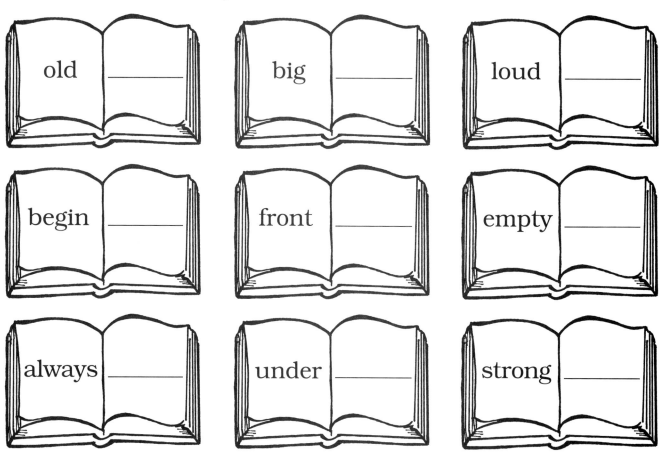

old _____   big _____   loud _____

begin _____   front _____   empty _____

always _____   under _____   strong _____

GRADE BOOSTER!

Choose a pair of antonyms. Write a sentence using both words.

_____

Skills: identifying antonyms, matching

TRACKING DOWN HOMONYMS

Homonyms are words that sound the same but have different meanings.

Examples: The sun shone in the sky.

Mrs. Burns has one son.

The words **sun** and **son** are homonyms.

Circle the pair of homonyms in each sentence below. Write the words on the lines.

1. I will write with my right hand.

   _____

2. Yesterday one lucky person won a car.

   _____

3. Last week Grandma was too weak to get out of bed. _____

4. We ate at eight o'clock. _____

5. Manny knew that his dad wanted a new saw.

   _____

6. I got four muffins for Evan. _____

7. Sasha thinks our friend will arrive in an hour.

   _____

BEAUTIFUL BUTTERFLIES

Look at the words on each butterfly. If the words are synonyms, write **S** on the butterfly's body. If they are antonyms, write **A**. If they are homonyms, write **H**.

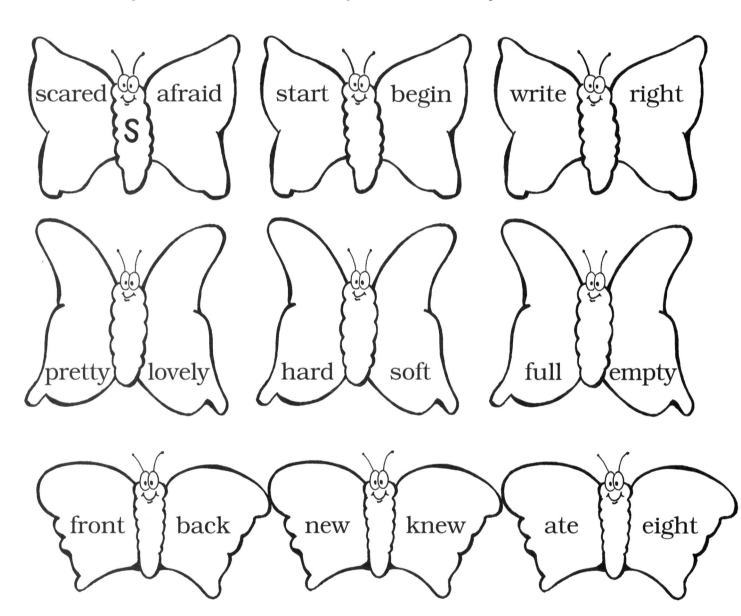

scared — afraid — **S**

start — begin

write — right

pretty — lovely

hard — soft

full — empty

front — back

new — knew

ate — eight

TOGETHER TIME: On a sheet of paper, make your own butterflies like the ones above. Ask a friend to write **S, A,** or **H** on the butterflies.

Skills: distinguishing synonyms, antonyms, and homonyms

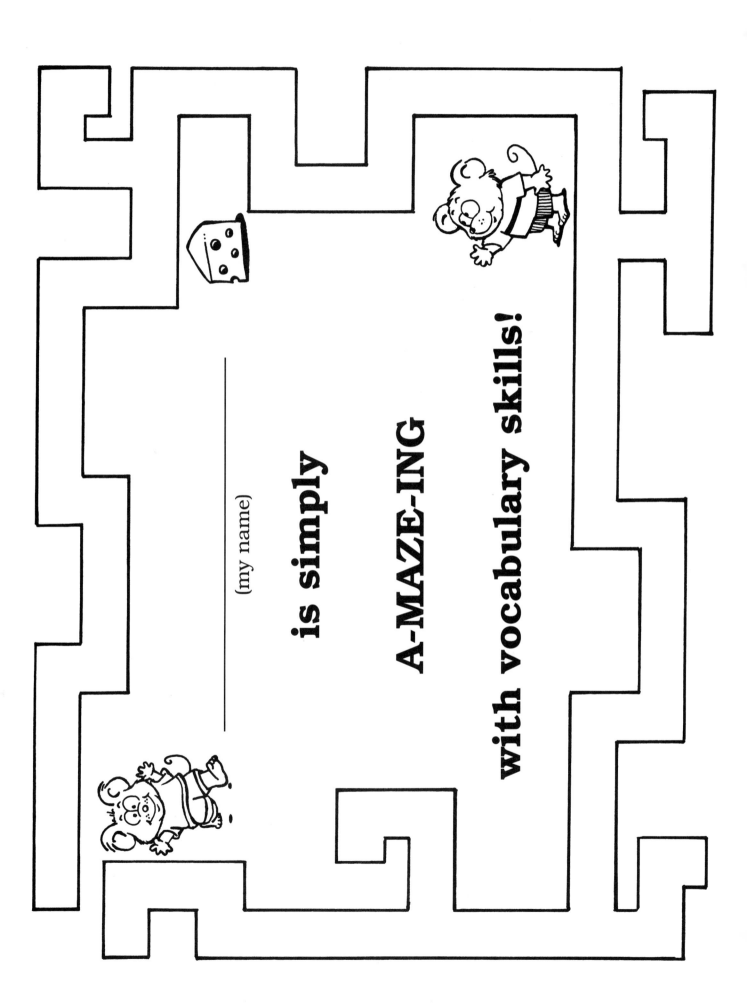

_____
(my name)

is simply

A-MAZE-ING

with vocabulary skills!

ALL ABOARD WITH NOUNS!

A **noun** is a word that names a person, a place, or a thing (such as **child, park,** or **wheel**).

Look at the trains. Replace the nouns in **bold** with three other nouns. Write your answers on the lines.

Let's go to the **store**.

The **king** spoke loudly.

My **book** is on the floor.

TOGETHER TIME: Write as many nouns as you can that name what you see around you. Ask a friend or a family member to do the same thing. At the end of a minute, compare your lists.

Skills: recognizing and writing nouns

BLAST OFF WITH PROPER NOUNS!

A **proper noun** names a particular person, place, or thing (such as **Linda, Mars,** or **Sunday**). Proper nouns begin with a capital letter.

Write a proper noun for each word below. Use words on the rocket.

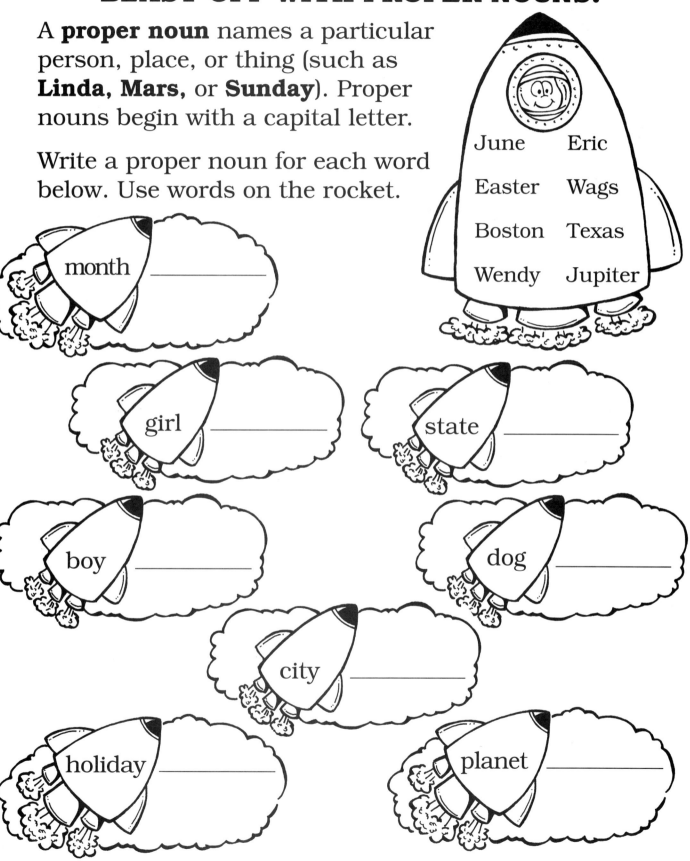

June   Eric

Easter   Wags

Boston   Texas

Wendy   Jupiter

month _____

girl _____

state _____

boy _____

dog _____

city _____

holiday _____

planet _____

ANIMALS IN ACTION

A **verb** is a word that usually describes an action, such as **walk** or **run**.

Circle the verbs in the poem. Write them on the lines.

Snakes wiggle,   _____

Ducks glide.   _____

Rabbits hop,   _____

And penguins slide. _____

Owls hoot,   _____

Eagles soar,   _____

Horses trot,   _____

And lions roar.   _____

Draw a picture of one of the animals from the poem.

Skills: identifying and writing verbs

SCHOOL NEWS

A **verb** often names an action, such as **walk** or **run**. When a verb tells about one noun (person, place, or thing), it usually ends in **s**. When it tells about more than one noun, it usually does not end in **s**.

Example: The boy **reads**. The boys **read**.

Write the correct verb form in each sentence.

1. (ride, rides) Kim _____ a bike to school.

2. (drive, drives) Some teachers _____ their cars.

3. (check, checks) Mr. Li _____ my work each day.

4. (visit, visits) The principal _____ our class sometimes.

5. (play, plays) Some children _____ ball at recess.

6. (drink, drinks) My friend _____ milk for lunch.

7. (practice, practices) They _____ math a lot.

8. (clean, cleans) Anna _____ her desk every day.

GRADE BOOSTER!

Write a sentence that tells one thing you and your classmates do at school.

_____

Skills: subject/verb agreement, verb forms

FUN AT CAMP

A verb that describes something that happened in the past often ends in **ed**. If a verb ends in silent **e,** you must drop the final **e** before adding **ed** to make the past tense.

Examples: play – play**ed**   bake – bak**ed**

Fill in the blanks. Add **ed** to the words under the lines.

1. The children _____ by bus to the campsite.
   travel

2. They _____ their suitcases in the cabins.
   unpack

3. Some children _____ along a rocky path.
   hike

4. Kirk and Dan _____ across the lake.
   row

5. A few children _____ in the water.
   wade

6. Some campers _____ a wooded area.
   explore

7. Lee's friends _____ to go fishing.
   decide

8. All the children _____ camping.
   enjoy

GRADE BOOSTER!

Write three verbs that tell what you did yesterday.

_____   _____   _____

Skills: writing the past tense of verbs using **ed,** comprehension

PUZZLING VERBS

Verbs that tell what happened in the past usually end in **ed,** such as **played**. Some verbs, though, have special forms for describing the past. For example, the past tense of **run** is **ran**.

Read the clues and fill in the puzzle with the past tense of each verb. Use the words in the box to help you.

Across

1. leave
3. hear
6. write
7. see
9. give
10. make
11. take

Down

1. lose
2. think
4. rise
5. swim
8. go

saw	swam
rose	wrote
lost	took
went	left
made	heard
gave	thought

A FOREST OF ADJECTIVES

An **adjective** is a word that describes a noun (a person, a place, or a thing).

Examples: The trees are **tall**.

A **hungry** bear looked for food.

The words **tall** and **hungry** are adjectives.

Look at the adjectives below. Write each one beside the noun it best describes.

deep   wooden   smooth   leafy

furry   scaly   grassy   prickly

_____ rabbit   _____ river

_____ field   _____ porcupine

_____ pebble   _____ cabin

_____ tree   _____ snake

Write a sentence describing something in the forest.

_____

_____

Skills: distinguishing adjectives, reasoning

RAY'S DREAM

An **adjective** describes a noun
(a person, a place, or a thing).
Read the sentences below.
Circle the adjectives. Write
them on the lines.

1. Ray had a strange dream. _____

2. He dreamed of a friendly dragon. _____

3. The dragon had gigantic wings. _____

4. It gave Ray a ride on its long back. _____

5. The amazing dragon soared upward. _____

6. A sleek jet sped by. _____

7. The surprised dragon swerved, and Ray fell.

   _____

8. When Ray woke up, he was on the cold floor beside
   his bed. _____

GRADE BOOSTER!

*On another sheet of paper, write three sentences
describing an imaginary creature. Use at least three
adjectives in your description. Circle the adjectives.*

Skills: identifying and writing adjectives

Parts of Speech Review

GETTING HOME

Help the children get home.
Look at the words on the path.
Then color each space according
to the code in the box.

CODE
noun — blue
proper noun — red
verb — yellow
adjective — green

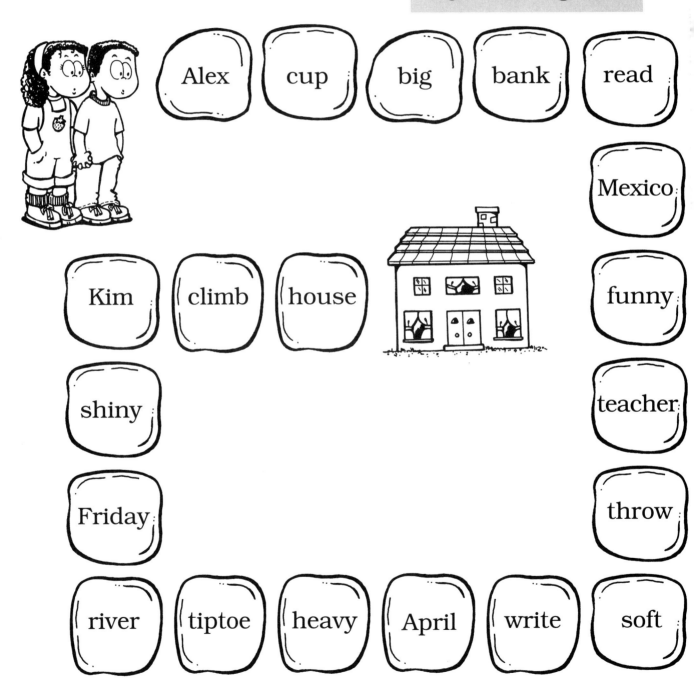

Alex cup big bank read Mexico funny teacher throw soft write April heavy tiptoe river Friday shiny Kim climb house

Skills: demonstrating mastery of different parts of speech

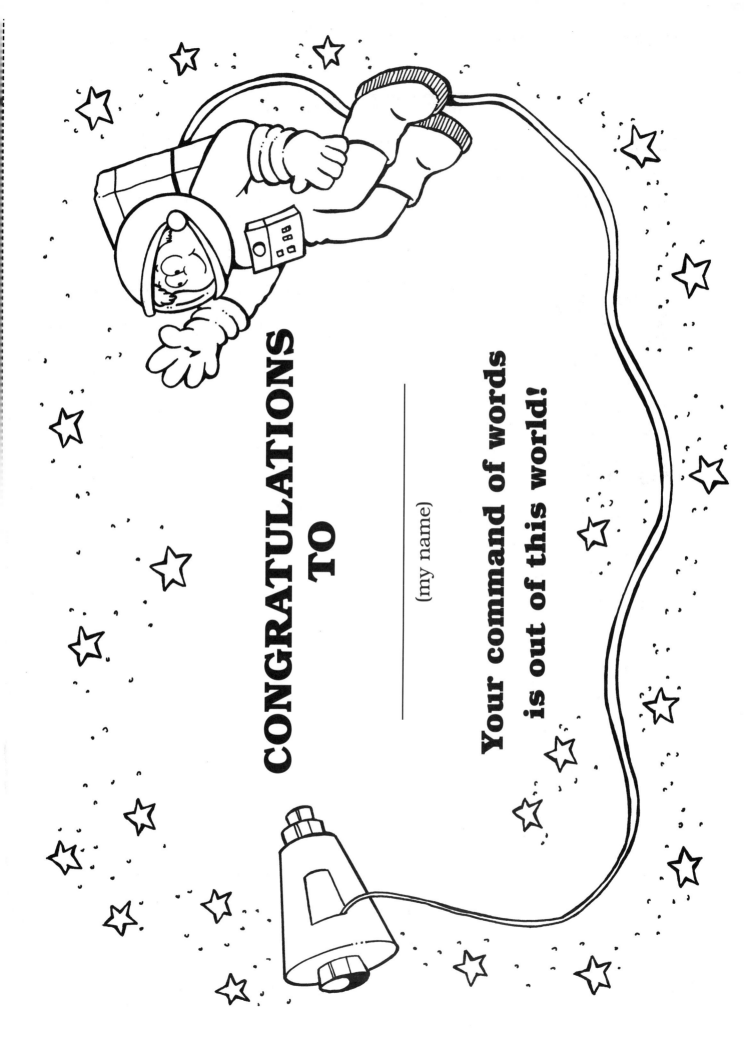

CONGRATULATIONS TO

(my name)

**Your command of words
is out of this world!**

CREEPY CRAWLIES

A sentence is a complete thought.

Examples: A spider has eight legs.

Eight legs.

The first example is a sentence because it tells you that a spider has eight legs. The second example is **not** a sentence because it does not give you a complete thought about eight legs.

Read each set of words. Write **yes** if the words form a sentence. Write **no** if they do not.

1. Ants are strong for their size. _____

2. Small ladybugs. _____

3. Snails have shells. _____

4. Feeds on leaves. _____

5. In hives. _____

6. A centipede has many legs. _____

7. Spins a web. _____

8. Some caterpillars are colorful. _____

TOGETHER TIME: Ask an adult to help you look outside for bugs and other small creatures. Make a list of what you find. Count how many different animals you see.

Skills: distinguishing between complete and incomplete sentences

AT THE BEACH

Every sentence has a **subject**. The subject is **who** or **what** the sentence is about.

Examples: **A girl** has a beach ball.

The sun shone brightly.

In the first sentence, the subject tells who has a beach ball. In the second sentence, the subject tells what shone brightly.

Circle the subject of each sentence.

1. A boy scooped up some sand.

2. The beach umbrella was orange.

3. Seagulls flew overhead.

4. Many people swam in the ocean.

5. A girl built a sand castle.

6. A sailboat glided in the water.

Complete each sentence by writing a subject.

_____ had bright stripes.

_____ lay on the sand.

_____ splashed in the water.

LET'S PLAY MUSIC

Every sentence has a **predicate**. The predicate describes the subject. It often tells what the subject is or does.

Example: Mark **plays the banjo**.

The predicate is **plays the banjo**. The words tell what Mark does.

Circle the predicate in each sentence.

1. Tamara takes piano lessons.

2. My uncle is a good guitar player.

3. Gretchen plays the flute.

4. The violin is a stringed instrument.

5. The children beat their drums.

6. The piano has black and white keys.

Draw lines to match the predicates on the right with the subjects on the left.

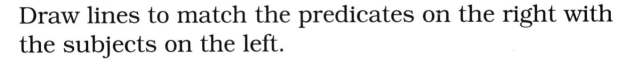

The trumpet   meets every Friday.

The music teacher   is made of brass.

The school band   waved a baton.

CHECK THE ORDER

The order of words affects the meaning of a sentence. For example:

The frog jumped over the boy.

The boy jumped over the frog.

In the first sentence, the frog does the jumping. In the second sentence, the boy does the jumping.

Write the sentence that describes each picture.

Tina is behind Jake.

Jake is behind Tina.

The girl hits the ball.

The ball hits the girl.

_____

_____

The baby sees a dog.

The dog sees a baby.

The cat is under the table.

The table is under the cat.

_____

_____

TELLING AND ASKING

A sentence can **tell** you something or it can **ask** you something. You can sometimes change the order of words to turn a sentence that tells into a sentence that asks.

Example: **It is** raining.

Is it raining?

Turn the sentences below into questions by changing the word order. Don't forget capital letters and question marks!

1. The sky is gray.

   _____

2. There are puddles everywhere.

   _____

3. The children are wearing raincoats.

   _____

4. A boy is carrying an umbrella.

   _____

GRADE BOOSTER!

On a sheet of paper, write one sentence that tells and another sentence that asks about the weather.

Skills: changing statements into questions, comprehension

JOINING SENTENCES

Sometimes you can use the word **and** to join two sentences.

Examples:

I ate a cookie. I ate an apple.

I ate a cookie **and** an apple.

I stayed at home. I played with my dog.

I stayed at home **and** I played with my dog.

Join the pairs of sentences with **and**. Rewrite the sentences on the lines.

1. We have one dog. We have two cats.

   _____

2. The truck is shiny. The truck is red.

   _____

3. Maria went shopping. She bought a coat.

   _____

4. The house is old. The house needs repairs.

   _____

5. Antonio likes horses. Diana likes turtles.

   _____

BIRD-WATCHING

You can make sentences more interesting by using "colorful" words.

Example:

The penguin walked on the ice.

The penguin **waddled** on the ice.

Waddled gives you a better idea of how the penguin moved because it "paints a picture" in your mind.

Write a colorful word for each **bold** word. Choose words from the box.

darted	sipped	strutted	cooed
glided	soared	screeched	flapped

1. The eagle **flew** high in the sky. _____

2. The swan **moved** across the water. _____

3. The owl **called** loudly. _____

4. The roadrunner **ran** across the road. _____

5. The ostrich **moved** its wings. _____

6. The peacock **walked** across the grass. _____

7. The pigeon **talked** softly. _____

8. The hummingbird **drank** sweet nectar. _____

Skills: identifying words that are more clear and exact, comprehension

CIRCUS ACTS

Write two sentences that describe each picture. Remember to:

• Begin each sentence with a capital letter.

• End each sentence with a period.

• Use colorful words.

A SENSIBLE ORDER

When you write a story, you have to write the sentences in an order that makes sense. Read the example below:

> Billy put on his skis. He started skiing at the sound of the signal. He reached the end of the course in less than a minute!

Write the sentences in order so that they tell a story.

Monica got on the plane.

She went to the airport.

Monica packed her suitcase.

_____

_____

_____

Jamal hung the shirt in his closet.

He put the shirt into the dryer.

Jamal washed his shirt.

_____

_____

_____

Skills: sequencing and writing sentences

A TOUCH OF CHOCOLATE

Imagine that you woke up one morning and found that everything you touched turned to chocolate! Write a story telling what happened. To help you plan your story, first answer these questions.

How did you feel? _____

Who did you talk to first? _____

What did you do? _____

How long did the chocolate touch last? _____

Write your story on the lines. Continue on another sheet of paper if you like.

_____

_____

_____

_____

_____

_____

_____

CHECK YOUR LANGUAGE SKILLS

Read the words below. Write **yes** if the words form a sentence. Write **no** if they do not.

The big cat is sleeping. _____

The clown puppet in the box. _____

Read the sentences below. For each sentence, circle the subject and underline the predicate.

The leaves fell slowly to the ground.

Some children played on the swings.

A duck swam in the pond.

Change the word order to turn the sentences below into questions.

The car is in the garage.

_____

There are coins on the table.

_____

Join this pair of sentences with **and**.

Sue bought some corn. Sue bought some carrots.

_____

Skills: identifying parts of sentences, rewriting sentences

WHAT AN OUTSTANDING PERFORMANCE!

_____

(my name)

is

terrific with sentences!

EXTRA!
EXTRA!
Read all about it!

_____
(my name)

is a
language arts
SENSATION!

Reading

This section offers children the opportunity to review consonants and vowels, both long and short, and their associated sounds. Word recognition is integrated with understanding overall concepts and ideas to strengthen comprehension skills. Children will complete exercises dealing with synonyms, antonyms, homonyms, as well as compounds, rhyming words, plurals, contractions, and syllables. Reasoning skills are also taught and reinforced through classification, categorizing, and comparison exercises.

I am ready to
start reading!

CONSONANT CONNECTION

Look at each picture below. Then write the **consonant** that it starts with on the blank line. The first one is done for you.

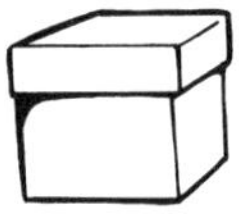    

B ______ ______ ______ ______ ______

______ ______ ______ ______ ______

______ ______ ______ ______ ______

    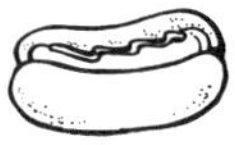

______ ______ ______ ______ ______

B	C	D	F	G	H	J	K	L	M	N	P	Q	R	S	T	V	W	X	Y	Z
b	c	d	f	g	h	j	k	l	m	n	p	q	r	s	t	v	w	x	y	z

GRADE BOOSTER!

*Which two **consonants** are not pictured above? ______ Can you think of words that begin with each of those **consonants**? On a separate piece of paper, write each word and then use it in a sentence.*

Skills: review of consonant recognition, discrimination, creativity

PIES AND CAKES

Do you remember the **long vowel rule**? Well, here it is:

The **long vowel** says its name! When a word has **two** vowels together, the first vowel is **long** and the second vowel is **silent**.

Match the words in the Word Box to their **long vowel** sounds by writing each word under its correct sound.

WORD BOX

rain	feet	fire	kite	tail	rake
bee	slide	pea	seal	baby	child

long ā as in cake

long ē as in tree

long ī as in pie

_____   _____   _____

_____   _____   _____

_____   _____   _____

_____   _____   _____

A SUIT AND A BOAT

Match the words in the Word Box to their **long vowel** sounds by writing each word under its correct sound.

WORD BOX

soap

music

toe

bone

fruit

note

cute

juice

long ō
as in
boat

_____   _____

_____   _____

_____   _____

_____   _____

Did you know that the consonant **Y** makes two different vowel sounds when it appears at the end of a word? It makes the **long ī** sound or the **long ē** sound. Draw a line from each word to the vowel sound it makes.

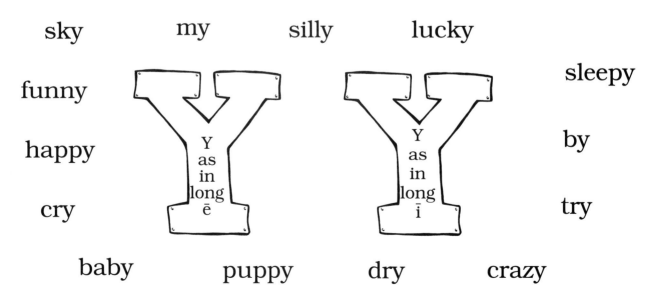

sky   my   silly   lucky

funny   sleepy

happy   by

cry   try

baby   puppy   dry   crazy

APPLES FOR INSECTS

Now it's time to review the **short vowel** sounds. Match the words in the Word Box to their **short vowel** sounds by writing each word under its correct sound. But be careful! There are some long vowel words hiding in the Word Box!

WORD BOX

pin	cat	tent	swim
nest	eel	mitten	man
bed	pan	kite	airplane

short ă as in apple

short ĕ as in bell

short ĭ as in insect

_____

_____

_____

_____

_____

_____

_____

_____

_____

_____

_____

_____

Skills: identifying and associating short vowel sounds, auditory discrimination, deduction

A ROCKIN' FROG

Match the words in the Word Box to their **short vowel** sounds by writing each word under its correct sound. But be careful! There are some long vowel words hiding in the Word Box!

WORD BOX

sun

box

doll

boot

skunk

nut

toe

octopus

short ǒ
as in frog

short ǔ
as in
duck

_____ _____

_____ _____

_____ _____

_____ _____

GRADE BOOSTER!

*On a separate piece of paper, write a story about a frog and a duck who live in a pond. Tell about all the wonderful adventures they have together. Use at least two **short ǒ** words and two **short ǔ** words in your story.*

REVIEW: Long and Short Vowels

Match each word in the Word Box to its correct picture by writing the word below its picture. Then write the **long** or **short vowel** sound that each word makes on the line provided. Some words may have more than one vowel sound. Then use crayons to color the long vowel words red and the short vowel words blue.

_____
(vowel sound)

_____
(vowel sound)

_____
(vowel sound)

_____
(vowel sound)

_____
(vowel sound)

_____
(vowel sound)

_____
(vowel sound)

_____
(vowel sound)

_____
(vowel sound)

_____
(vowel sound)

_____
(vowel sound)

_____
(vowel sound)

WORD BOX

| baby | rain | cat | slide | skunk | cane |
| jet | smoke | mop | key | cube | puppy |

Skills: demonstrating mastery of long and short vowel sounds through review

THE FROG ARTIST

The **R blend** is a consonant combined with the letter **R** to make a special sound.

Frederick likes to **dr**aw with **cr**ayons. Use your favorite color **cr**ayon to **dr**aw a line **fr**om each **R blend** to the picture that it des**cr**ibes.

cr

dr

tr

gr

fr

pr

br

GRADE BOOSTER!

*Which **R blend** has the most pictures above?* _____
*Which **R blend** has the least pictures above?* _____

Skills: identifying and associating R consonant blends, auditory and visual discrimination

THE CLOUD-RIDING CLOWN

The **L blend** is a consonant combined with the letter **L** to make a special sound.

sl	cl	bl	fl	pl	gl

Read the sentence below. Circle all the words that begin with an **L blend**.

Clarice the Clown needs glasses to see clearly through the clouds.

Now help Clarice write the **L blend** words below in alphabetical (ABC) order on the blank lines.

blocks   glasses   plane   slide   sleep

flower   flag   blanket   clock

_____ _____ _____

_____ _____ _____

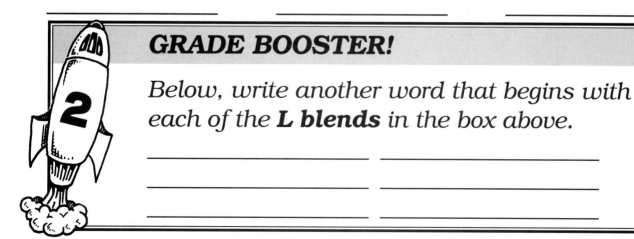

GRADE BOOSTER!

*Below, write another word that begins with each of the **L blends** in the box above.*

_____ _____

_____ _____

_____ _____

SPLISH-SPLASHIN' SHAWN

> The **S blend** is a consonant combined with the letter **S** to make a special sound.

Shawn **sp**lashes into the pool of **S blends**. Help him connect each picture to its beginning **S blend** sound by drawing a line between them.

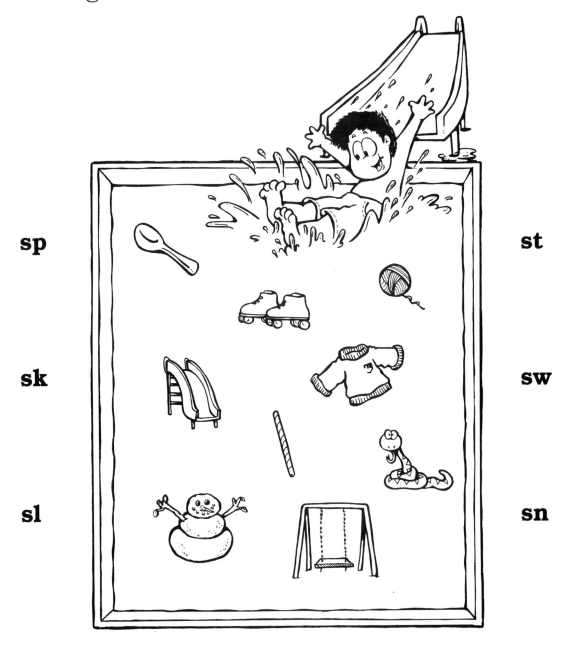

sp   st

sk   sw

sl   sn

Skills: identifying and associating S consonant blends, auditory and visual discrimination

CHUCKY'S SHOE

A **digraph** is a combination of two different letters that together make a single sound.

Read the following sentence and then circle all the words that contain digraphs of the letter **H**.

Chucky the Chipmunk chuckled and shrieked when he got his shoe caught in the wheel.

Now draw a line connecting each word with the digraph it contains.

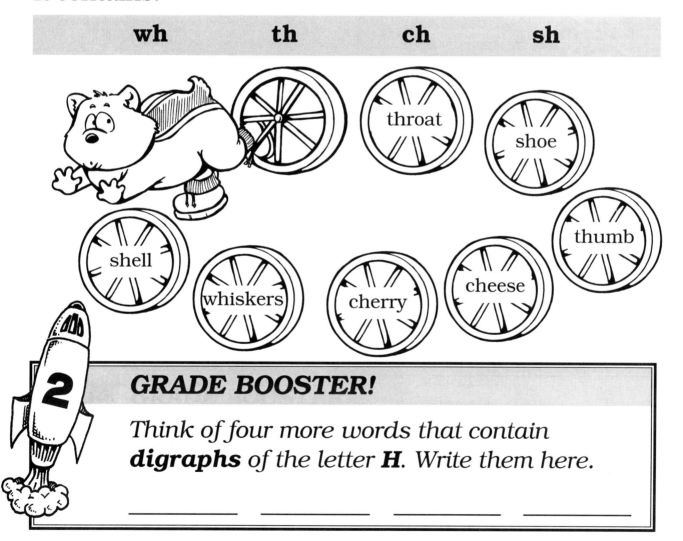

wh   **th**   **ch**   **sh**

throat

shoe

thumb

shell

whiskers

cherry

cheese

GRADE BOOSTER!

Think of four more words that contain **digraphs** *of the letter* **H***. Write them here.*

_____ _____ _____ _____

REVIEW: Consonant Blends and Digraphs

Circle each consonant blend or digraph that goes with each picture.

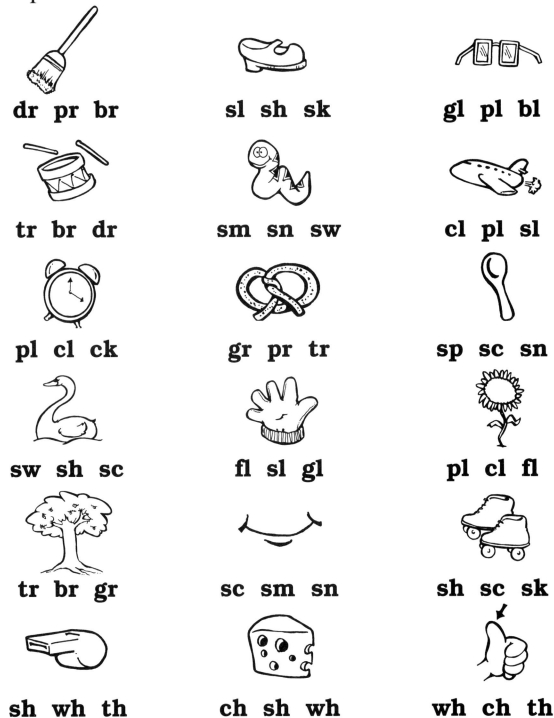

dr pr br   sl sh sk   gl pl bl

tr br dr   sm sn sw   cl pl sl

pl cl ck   gr pr tr   sp sc sn

sw sh sc   fl sl gl   pl cl fl

tr br gr   sc sm sn   sh sc sk

sh wh th   ch sh wh   wh ch th

Skills: demonstrating mastery of consonant blends and digraphs through review

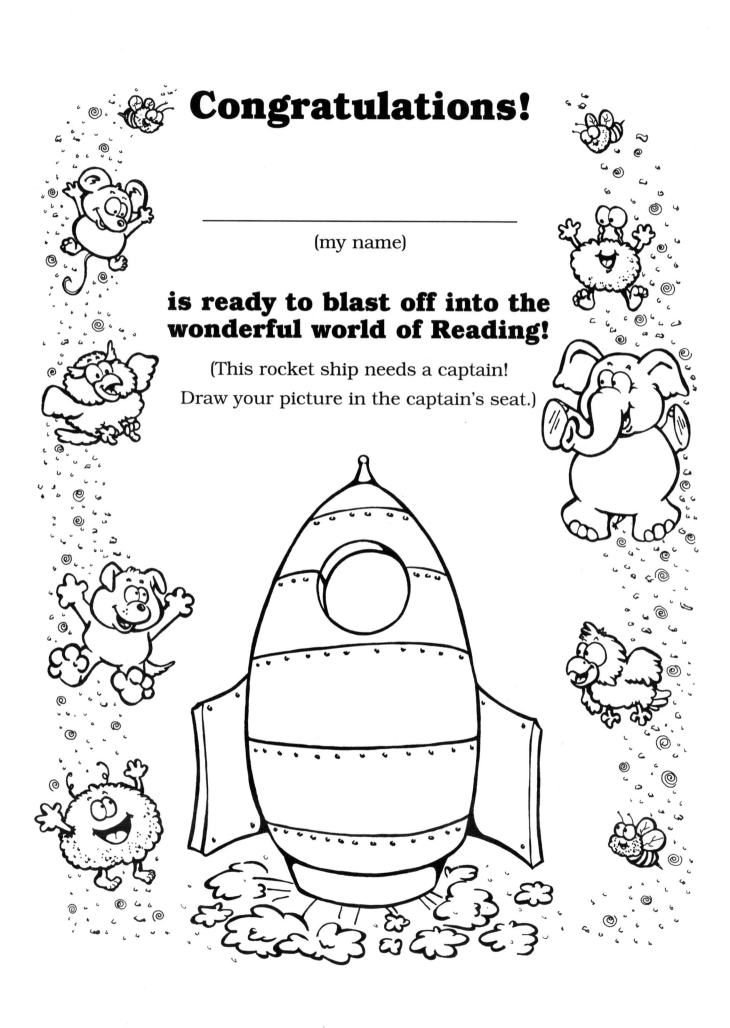

Congratulations!

_____

(my name)

is ready to blast off into the wonderful world of Reading!

(This rocket ship needs a captain!
Draw your picture in the captain's seat.)

THE GREAT SYNONYM MATCH

Words that mean the same or close to the same thing are called **synonyms**. Draw a line from each word on the left side of each book to its **synonym** on the right side. The first word is done for you.

Skills: introducing and reinforcing synonyms, reasoning, deduction

SYNONYM SQUARES

Circle the **synonym** on each square that has the same meaning or close to the same meaning as the word in **bold** print. The first one is done for you.

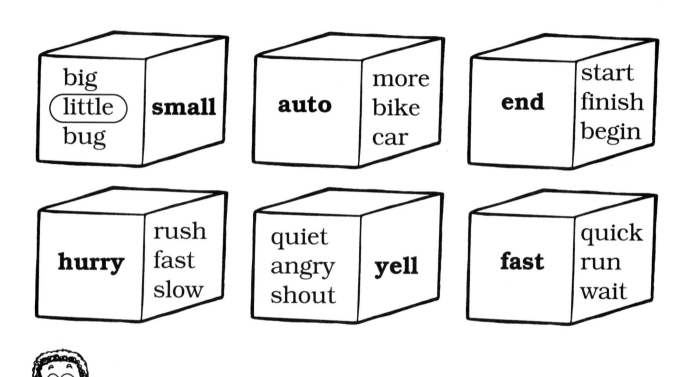

TOGETHER TIME: Ask an adult to help you think of a **synonym** for each of the following words. Write the **synonym** on the line provided. When you're done, grab another piece of paper and use each **synonym** in a sentence.

exam _____	scared _____
large _____	friend _____
maybe _____	fall _____
choose _____	high _____

Skills: reinforcing synonyms, reasoning, deduction, creativity

TEETER-TOTTER OPPOSITES

Words that mean the opposite of each other are called **antonyms**. You probably already know lots of **antonyms**. Use the words in the Word Box to help you find the opposite of the words on the teeter-totters. Then write each **antonym** on the teeter-totter next to its opposite. A few have been done for you.

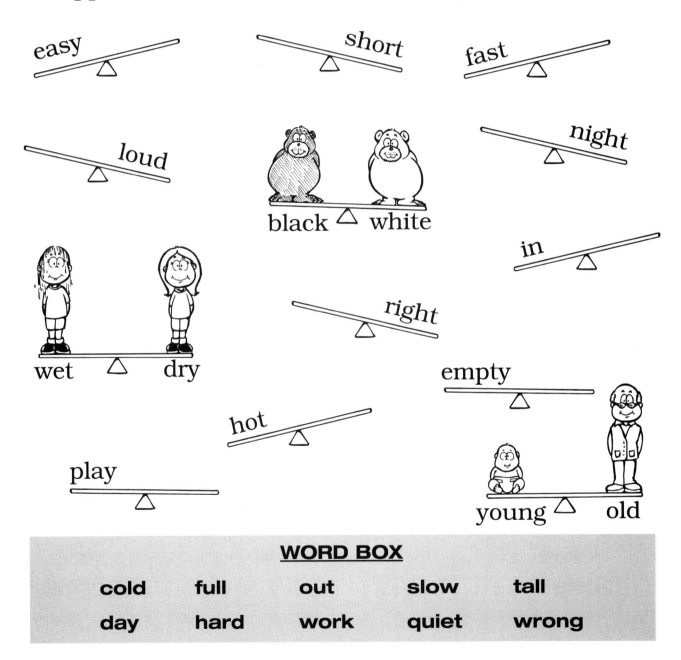

WORD BOX

cold	full	out	slow	tall
day	hard	work	quiet	wrong

Skills: introducing and reinforcing antonyms, reasoning, deduction

ANDY AND ALLIE

Andy and Allie always do the opposite of each other. When Andy feels cold, Allie is hot. Complete the sentences below so that Andy and Allie always act just like **antonyms**—the opposite of each other.

1. When Andy opens the window,

   Allie _____ it.

2. Allie's room is very _____, but Andy's room is dirty.

3. Andy walks near the water, but

   Allie stays _____ from it.

4. Allie turns the light off, but Andy turns it

   _____.

5. Allie has a big dog, but Andy

   has a _____ one.

A GARDEN OF WORDS

Let's review our **synonyms** (same) and **antonyms** (opposite). Use crayons to color the flowers with **synonyms** yellow and the flowers with **antonyms** red.

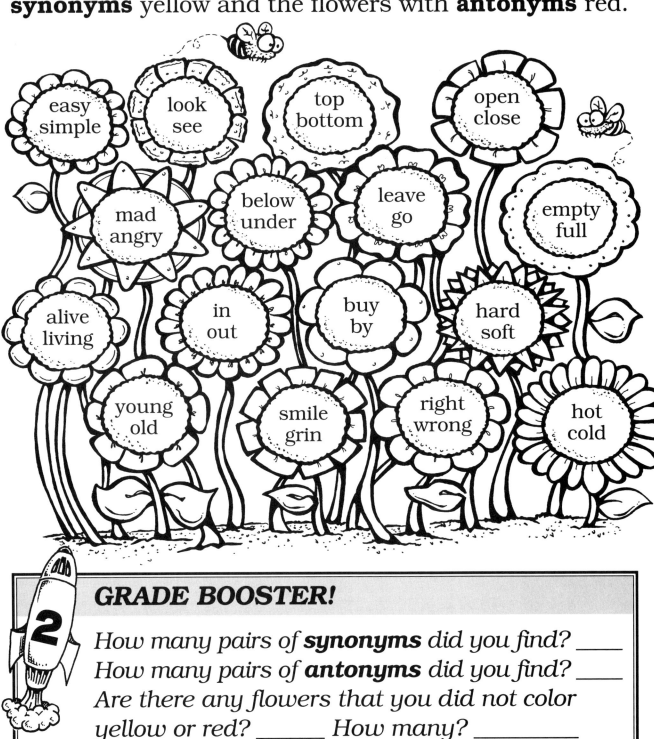

GRADE BOOSTER!

*How many pairs of **synonyms** did you find? _____*
*How many pairs of **antonyms** did you find? _____*
Are there any flowers that you did not color yellow or red? _____ How many? _____

HOMONYM HUNT

Homonyms are words that sound alike but are spelled differently and have different meanings. Match the words in the Word Box to their **homonyms** by writing them under their **homonyms** in the balls. The first one is done for you.

WORD BOX

blue	male	road	tail	heel	meet	sail	to
here	no	not	so	hole	way	some	write

two
to

blew
_____

knot
_____

meat
_____

mail
_____

weigh
_____

sum
_____

heal
_____

know
_____

sew
_____

whole
_____

hear
_____

rode
_____

right
_____

sale
_____

tale
_____

Skills: introducing and reinforcing homonyms, visual discrimination, creativity

87

TO THE BEACH

Follow the path from the parking lot to the beach by writing the **homonym** for each word on the line below it. Use the Word Box to help you.

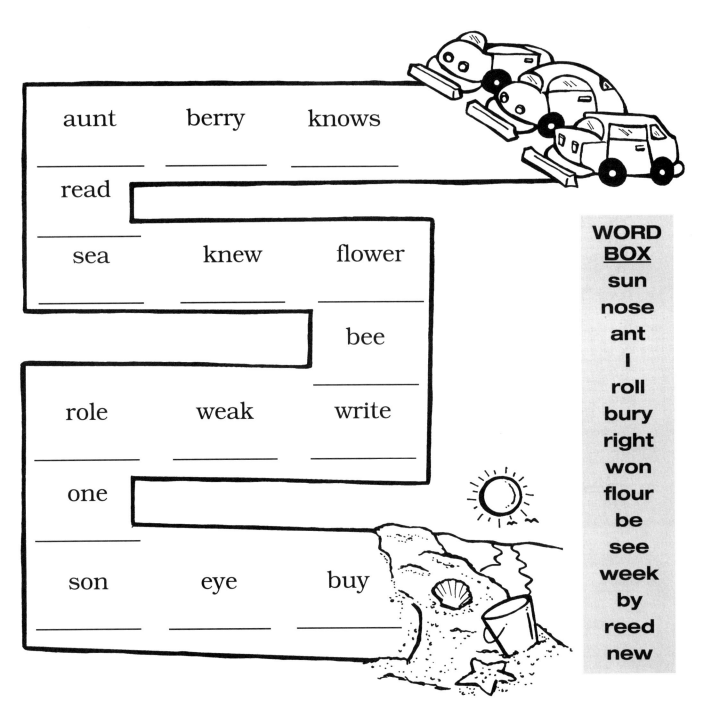

aunt   berry   knows

_____   _____   _____

read

_____

sea   knew   flower

_____   _____

bee

role   weak   write

_____   _____   _____

one

_____

son   eye   buy

_____   _____   _____

WORD BOX

sun
nose
ant
I
roll
bury
right
won
flour
be
see
week
by
reed
new

Skills: reinforcing homonyms, visual discrimination

THE HOARSE HORSE

Circle the **homonyms** in the following sentences:

Hal the horse has had a sore throat all week. His voice has been hoarse and weak. So instead of running around the fields, he has been lounging on the grass watching the birds soar through the sky.

How many pairs of **homonyms** did you find? _____

Now read each sentence below. If the word in **bold** print makes sense in the sentence, put **OK** on the line next to it. If the **bold** word does not make sense, write a word that does on the line. The first two are done for you.

- The policeman **blue** his whistle. *blew*
- There was a **knot** in the rope. OK
- I like to eat **pairs**. _____
- The **night** is very cold and dark.

  _____
- Do you **know** all the letters of the alphabet? _____
- Please give me a **peace** of candy. _____
- How much do you **way**? _____
- There are **eight** people in my family.

  _____

Skills: reinforcing homonyms, visual discrimination, deduction

REVIEW: Synonyms, Antonyms, and Homonyms

Fill in the word that best fits each description below. When you are done, circle each of your answers in the word search. The words in the word search can go up (↑), down (↓), or sideways (→).

- Opposite of **night**: _____
- Antonym of **beautiful**: _____
- Synonym of **center**: _____
- Opposite of **black**: _____
- Homonym of **bury**: _____
- Homonym of **knows**: _____
- Antonym of **strong**: _____
- Homonym of **whole**: _____
- Means the same as **correct**: _____
- Homonym of **won**: _____
- Means the same as **child**: _____
- Antonym of **cold**: _____

```
t  r  m  v  n  c  d  f  g  i  v  t  i  p
l  i  e  q  o  b  k  h  b  x  s  o  n  e
o  g  e  p  w  h  i  t  e  d  v  h  o  s
e  h  o  l  e  o  d  n  r  w  o  k  s  n
p  t  l  d  a  y  m  l  r  g  c  j  e  u
n  s  o  n  k  u  g  l  y  z  d  b  m  r
q  r  k  m  s  j  k  a  m  i  d  d  l  e
```

Skills: demonstrating mastery of words through review, discrimination

When it comes to knowing Synonyms, Antonyms, and Homonyms

_____

(my name)

is

NUMBER ONE!

COMPOUND GLASSES

When two small words are put together to make one bigger word, that new word is called a **compound word**. Create **compound words** by combining the words in the eyeglasses. Write the **compound words** on the lines. Fill in the blanks where needed.

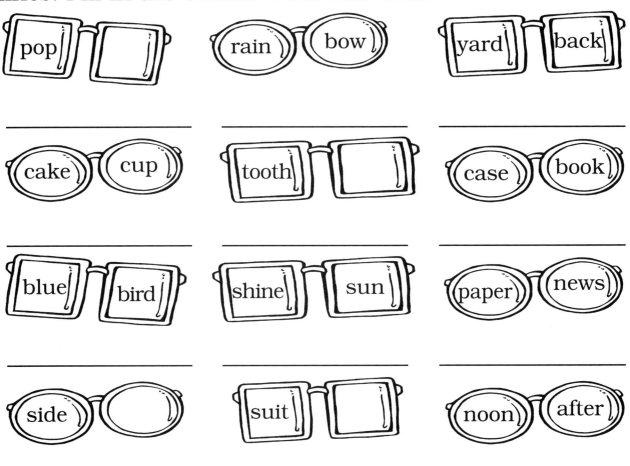

 *GRADE BOOSTER!*

2 *Make as many **compound words** as you can with the words below. Write each compound on a separate piece of paper.*

bath   front   side   cow   tooth

Skills: introducing and reinforcing compound words, deduction, creativity

COMPOUNDS UPON COMPOUNDS

Sometimes one word can be combined with many different words to make a few **compound words**. Look at each group of words below. Then find the word in the Word Box that could be combined with all the words in each group to make **compound words**. Write that word on the line provided. The first one is done for you.

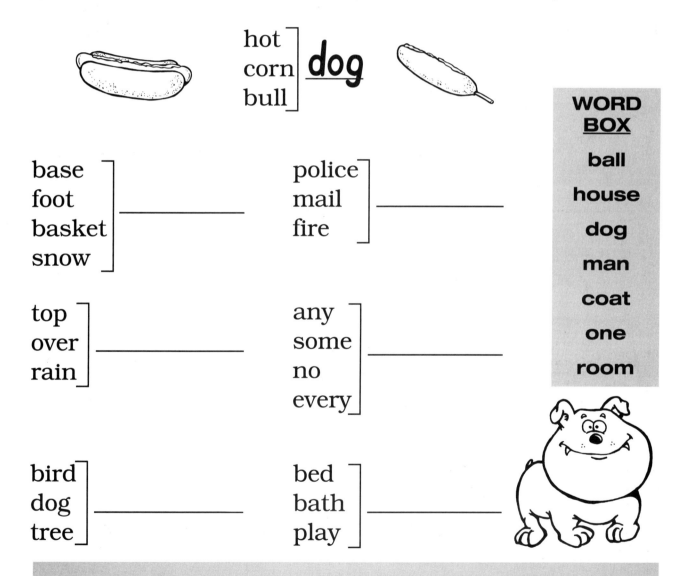

hot
corn **dog**
bull

WORD BOX

ball

house

dog

man

coat

one

room

base
foot
basket   _____
snow

police
mail   _____
fire

top
over   _____
rain

any
some
no   _____
every

bird
dog   _____
tree

bed
bath   _____
play

TOGETHER TIME: Ask an adult to help you alphabetize each group of words on a separate piece of paper.

THE PUP IN THE CUP

Rhyming words have the same ending sound. Look at the ending sounds in the confetti below. Then write two rhyming words for each ending on the lines provided.

ad
_____

ug
_____

op
_____

ar
_____

ot
_____

est
_____

et
_____

ell
_____

ox
_____

us
_____

in
_____

un
_____

ill
_____

GRADE BOOSTER!

*Look at the words below. Then find two words that **rhyme** with each one. Write them on the lines.*

ham _____   _____

mitt _____   _____

Skills: introducing and reinforcing rhyming words, auditory discrimination, creativity

BOOKS, BOOKS, AND MORE BOOKS

Singular words are words that mean one. **Plural words** are words that mean more than one. You can make most nouns **plural** by adding **s** to the end of the word. For example, the plural of **book** is **books** . Now write the **plural** forms of each **singular** word below.

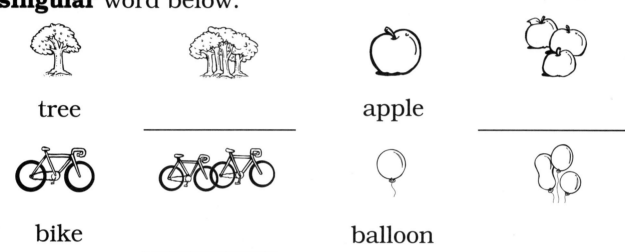

tree _____   apple _____

bike _____   balloon _____

If a noun ends with a consonant and then the letter **y,** you make it **plural** by changing the **y** to **i** and adding **es**. For example, the plural of the word **baby** is **babies** . Write the plural forms of the **singular** words below.

lady _____   candy _____

fly _____   family _____

DUAL DRESSES

When a singular noun ends in **s, ss, ch, sh, x,** or **z,** you add **es** to the end to make it plural. For example, the plural of the word **dress** is **dresses**. Write the **plural** forms of the words below.

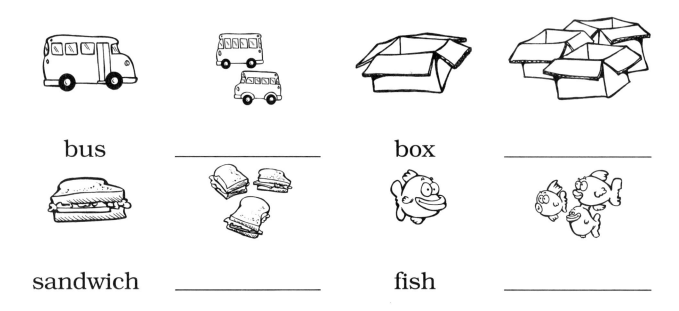

bus _____   box _____

sandwich _____   fish _____

Sometimes a word changes form when it becomes **plural**. Draw a line from each picture to the word that is its **plural**.

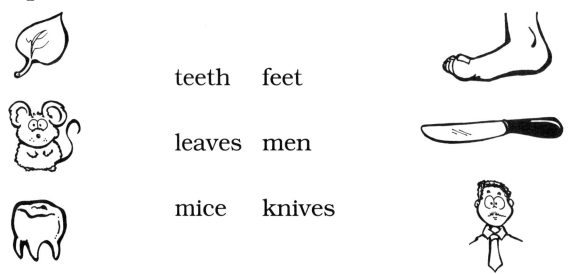

teeth   feet

leaves   men

mice   knives

BUTTERFLY CONTRACTIONS

Contractions are words that are formed when two small words are put together, but one or more letters are left out. The missing letters are replaced with an **apostrophe (')**.

Write the **contractions** formed when you combine each of the pairs of words below. The first one is done for you.

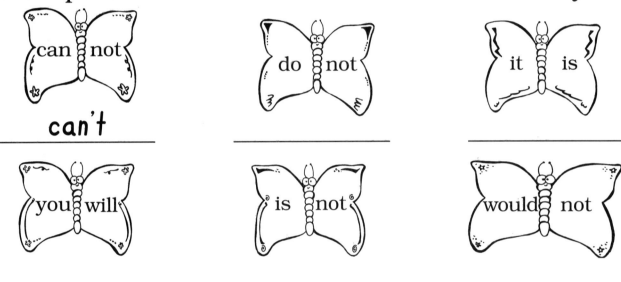

can't

Now write the two words that make up each contraction.

I'm   couldn't   she'll

that's   hasn't   wasn't

GRADE BOOSTER!

*On a separate piece of paper, write a sentence or question using each **contraction** above.*

Skills: introducing association of contractions with source words, creativity   **97**

LET'S USE CONTRACTIONS

Read the story below. Circle all of the contractions that you see. Then write each contraction and the two words that form the contraction on the lines below.

On Sunday morning, Jamie and her family were going to the zoo. Jamie couldn't wait. She hadn't been to the zoo before and she knew she'd love it. Her big brother Jeffrey told Jamie, "It's so much fun! You'll love the monkeys. They're so cute."

Jamie had a great time at the zoo. She didn't want to leave when the day was over. So her parents told her they'd be able to come back soon.

Contraction   Two Words

_____   _____

_____   _____

_____   _____

_____   _____

_____   _____

_____   _____

_____   _____

_____   _____

       Skills: reinforcing association of contractions with source words

SILLY SYLLABLES

Baxter is blowing bubbles. The words **bubbles** and **Baxter** each have two **syllables,** or parts: **bub–bles** and **Bax–ter**. Look at the words in the bubbles below. Say each word out loud. Then count the number of parts or **syllables** you hear. Write that number on the line below each word.

flower ____

soap ____

sleep ____

popcorn ____

remember ____

spelling ____

candy ____

laugh ____

rain ____

school ____

basketball ____

bear ____

house ____

different ____

funny ____

grandmother ____

bubbles ____

TOGETHER TIME: Ask an adult to help you find a single die around your house. Roll the die. Then say a word that has the same number of syllables as the number that appeared on the die. Then have your adult friend do the same thing. Keep taking turns until you each have said one word for each number on the die.

Skills: introducing and reinforcing syllables, spelling, deduction

SYL-LA-BLE SEN-SA-TION

Look at the words in the Word Box. Count the number of **syllables** in each word. Then write each word under the number that tells how many **syllables** it has.

WORD BOX					
milk	student	teacher	volleyball	bathtub	gum
grape	operator	mailman	professor	history	girl

1

2

3

_____   _____   _____

_____   _____   _____

_____   _____   _____

_____   _____   _____

GRADE BOOSTER!

Now put each list of words above in alphabetical order on the lines below. One word has four **syllables**. *Do you know which word? Write it here:* _____

1   **2**   **3**

_____   _____   _____

_____   _____   _____

_____   _____   _____

_____   _____   _____

Skills: reinforcing syllables, spelling, deduction, alphabetizing

REVIEW: Word Classification and Identification

Complete each of the following statements. Then write each of your answers in a blank bingo box below.

- The plural of **sandwich** is _____.

- The contraction of **cannot** is _____.

- The compound of **pop** and **corn** is _____.

- There is (are) _____ syllable(s) in the word **pipe**.

- The compound of **butter** and **fly** is _____.

- There are (is) _____ syllable(s) in the word **television**.

- The contraction of **do** and **not** is _____.

- The singular of **families** is _____.

	FREE	

TOGETHER TIME: Copy each of the answers above onto small pieces of paper and put them in a bowl or a hat. Then ask an adult to play a game of word bingo with you. Use buttons or other small round objects to cover the words as you play. As soon as you cover three words all in one row, yell BINGO!

_____

(my name)

is a
MASTER OF WORDS!

CLASSY CLASSIFICATION

Classifying means grouping words together that have similar meanings or something in common. Classify each group of words below. Draw a line matching each group to the one word in the center of the page that describes **all** the words in the group.

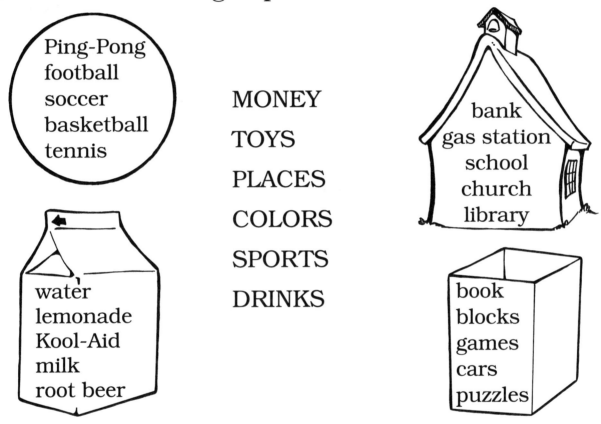

Ping-Pong
football
soccer
basketball
tennis

MONEY

TOYS

PLACES

COLORS

SPORTS

DRINKS

bank
gas station
school
church
library

water
lemonade
Kool-Aid
milk
root beer

book
blocks
games
cars
puzzles

Now complete each sentence with a word that tells or describes what the words in **bold** print have in common.

- **Apples** and **grapes** are _____.
- **Sally** and **Maria** are _____.
- **California** and **Texas** are _____.
- **Winter** and **summer** are _____.
- **Balls** and **wheels** are _____.

MORE CLASSIFYING

Let's practice more **classification**. Draw a line from each group of words to the one word in the center of the page that describes **all** the words in the group.

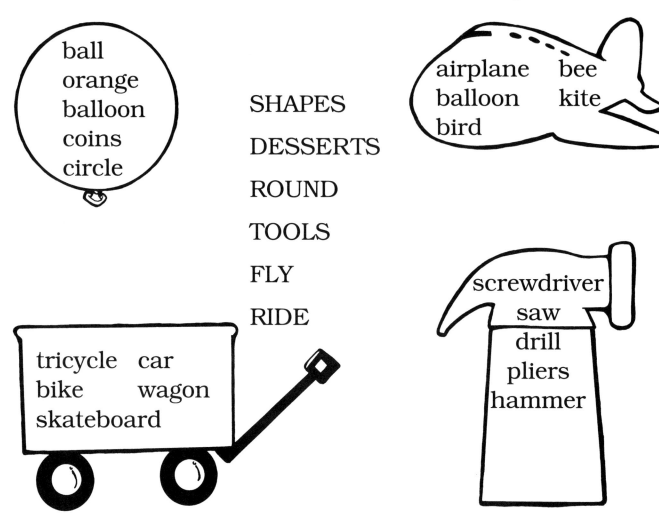

ball
orange
balloon
coins
circle

SHAPES

DESSERTS

ROUND

TOOLS

FLY

RIDE

airplane   bee
balloon   kite
bird

tricycle   car
bike   wagon
skateboard

screwdriver
saw
drill
pliers
hammer

Now complete each sentence with a word that tells or describes what the words in **bold** print have in common.

• **Ice cream** and **snow** are _____.
• **Puppies** and **kittens** are _____.
• **Plants** and **grass** are _____.
• **Dogs** and **fish** are _____.
• **Tomatoes** and **cucumbers** are _____.

MONTH MADNESS

Unscramble the twelve months of the year by writing them in the correct order on the lines below.

April	February	July	October	January	August
March	September	June	December	November	May

1. _____

2. _____

3. _____

4. _____

5. _____

6. _____

7. _____

8. _____

9. _____

10. _____

11. _____

12. _____

GRADE BOOSTER!

Now unscramble the seven days of the week and write them in the proper order on the lines below.

Tuesday   Thursday   Saturday   Friday
Sunday   Wednesday   Monday

1. _____

2. _____

3. _____

4. _____

5. _____

6. _____

7. _____

STAGELOFOLUS

Clever Charley created a character named Stagelofolus. Now show how clever you are by following the directions below to finish the picture. Use crayons to draw or color each part as indicated.

1. Put a hat on Stagelofolus. Color it brown.
2. Put three flowers to the right of Stagelofolus. Color one red, one blue, and one yellow.
3. Draw a small tree to the left of Stagelofolus. Color its leaves green.
4. Put a dog next to the tree and color it gray.
5. Draw a bird flying in the sky. Color the bird blue.
6. Put a round sun in the sky over the flowers. Color it yellow.

GRADE BOOSTER!

On a separate piece of paper, write a short story about Stagelofolus.

Skills: following directions, comprehension, recognizing details, creativity

A COUNTRY HOUSE

Create a country setting for this house by following the directions below to finish the picture. Use crayons to draw or color each part as indicated.

1. Draw green grass under and around the house.
2. Draw curtains in all the windows of the house.
3. Draw a pie sitting on the sill of the open window.
4. Put an apple tree to the right of the house. Color the leaves green, the apples red, and the tree trunk brown.
5. Draw a dirt path leading up to the front door.
6. Draw two children playing in the yard. Make one child a boy and one child an older girl.

GRADE BOOSTER!

On a separate piece of paper, write a short story about this country house. Who lives in the house? How long have they lived there?

CAUSE AND EFFECT

> **Cause:** An action or act that makes something happen.
> **Effect:** Something that happens because of an action or cause.

Look at the following example of **cause** and **effect**.

Your mother loves you. She takes good care of you.
      cause   **effect**

Now draw a line connecting each **cause** on the left side of the page to its **effect** on the right side of the page.

Skills: introducing and identifying cause and effect, reasoning, deduction

MORE EFFECTS

Draw a line connecting the pictures that go together. Then figure out which picture is the **cause** and which is the **effect**. Write **C** for **cause** or **E** for **effect** under each picture.

TOGETHER TIME: Ask an adult to help you think of three events that happened today. Why did they happen? Describe the **cause** and **effect** of each event. *Hint:* There may be more than one **cause** for each event.

Skills: identifying cause and effect, reasoning, deduction

FACT VS. OPINION

A **fact** is something that can be proven as true. An **opinion** is a person's belief or feeling. Read each statement below and decide if it is a **fact** (can prove it) or an **opinion** (someone's feeling). Write an **F** for **fact** or an **O** for **opinion** on the line next to each sentence.

- The ball is round. _____
- That is a cute dog. _____
- Mom works every day. _____
- Pizza tastes good. _____
- Playing at the park is fun. _____
- The car has a radio. _____
- Flowers smell good. _____
- The music is too loud. _____
- Laurie and Suzie are friends. _____

Yellowstone is the best place to camp.

I like the Grand Canyon much better.

GRADE BOOSTER!

*Change each **opinion** sentence to a **fact** sentence. Write each new sentence on a separate piece of paper.*

Skills: introducing and reinforcing fact vs. opinion, analysis, creativity

MORE FACTS AND OPINIONS

Look at the pictures below. Then write one **fact** (can prove it) sentence and one **opinion** (someone's feelings) sentence about each picture. One is done for you.

FACT: *The boy is reading the book.*
OPINION: *The boy likes the book he is reading.*

FACT: _____
_____
OPINION: _____
_____

FACT: _____
_____
OPINION: _____
_____

FACT: _____
_____
OPINION: _____
_____

Skills: reinforcing fact vs. opinion, analysis, creativity

REVIEW: Reasoning Skills

Fill in the crossword puzzle below. Use the words in the Word Box to help you.

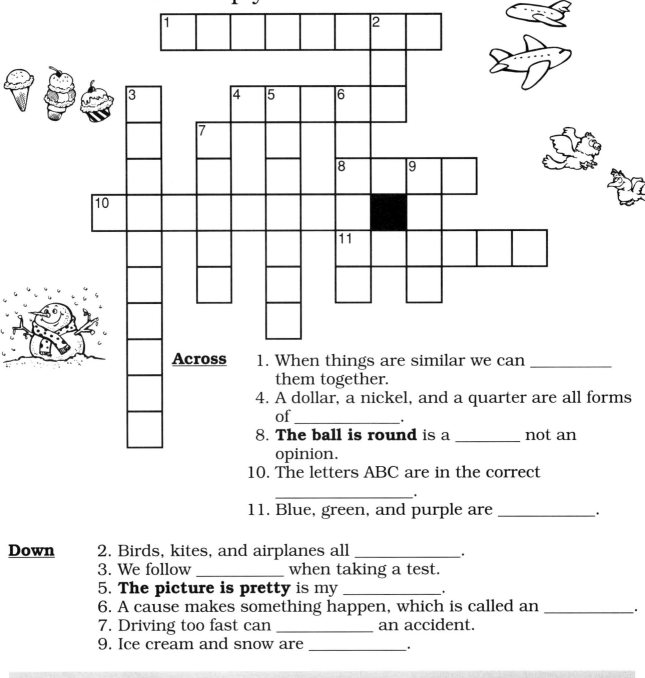

Across

1. When things are similar we can _____ them together.
4. A dollar, a nickel, and a quarter are all forms of _____.
8. **The ball is round** is a _____ not an opinion.
10. The letters ABC are in the correct _____.
11. Blue, green, and purple are _____.

Down

2. Birds, kites, and airplanes all _____.
3. We follow _____ when taking a test.
5. **The picture is pretty** is my _____.
6. A cause makes something happen, which is called an _____.
7. Driving too fast can _____ an accident.
9. Ice cream and snow are _____.

WORD BOX

directions	classify	fly	effect	fact	cold
sequence	cause	opinion	money	colors	

Skills: demonstrating mastery of reasoning skills through review

This certifies that

_____
(my name)

is a whiz at

Reasoning Skills

MARTY GETS THE MAIN IDEA

The **main idea** is what a story is about. Help Marty figure out the **main idea** of the passages below Write a check mark (✓) next to each main idea.

Finding the main idea is my game.

Chrissi's father is a policeman. He goes to work every day and wears a uniform. Sometimes he gives people tickets. Sometimes his job is dangerous.

____ Everyone likes policemen.

____ Chrissi's dad is a policeman.

____ Policemen help people.

There are many things that are green. Grass and leaves are green. A traffic signal is sometimes green. Many vegetables are green. Some money is green.

____ Vegetables are always green.

____ Green is a good color.

____ Many things are green.

I like to listen to music. It makes me happy. When I hear music, I want to tap my foot and dance. I like to sing along with the melody.

____ I sing to music.

____ I enjoy music.

____ I want to learn to play music.

Skills: comprehending the main idea, recognizing details

SARAH USES HER SENSES

Sarah uses all five of her senses every day. Help her figure out which part(s) of her body she uses with each sense. Draw a line matching each sense to the body part that relates to it.

sight

hearing

taste

touch

smell

Now draw a line matching each picture to the sense (or senses) that relates to it.

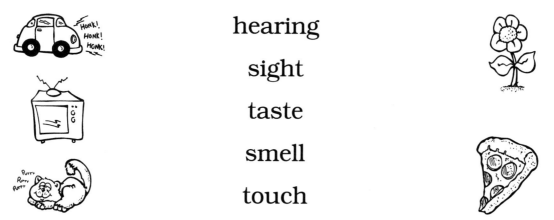

hearing

sight

taste

smell

touch

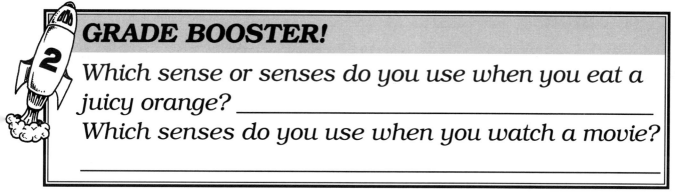

GRADE BOOSTER!

Which sense or senses do you use when you eat a juicy orange? _____

Which senses do you use when you watch a movie?

_____

Skills: drawing conclusions, identifying senses

FOOD FOR THOUGHT

Read the paragraph below. Then complete each statement that follows by underlining the phrase that makes the most sense. Use the information given as well as your own knowledge to help you make your choice. This choice is called your **conclusion**.

The chipmunk ran along the ground looking for food. He found a nut in the leaves. He stuffed it into his cheek. When his cheek was full of nuts, he hurried off to bury them in the ground near a tree. Then he went in search of more nuts. He buried those nuts, as well.

- The chipmunk was gathering nuts because (a) he was hungry; (b) he was playing a game; (c) he was storing them for the winter.

- This story takes place in (a) winter; (b) spring; (c) summer; (d) fall.

- In the winter, the chipmunk will probably (a) starve; (b) forget where he has stored his nuts; (c) have lots to eat.

Skills: drawing conclusions, comprehension

URSULA USES CONTEXT CLUES

Read each sentence below. Then help Ursula fill in the blank by circling the word that makes the most sense. The other words in the sentence, called the **context,** will help you figure out which word fits best.

Dad wants to buy Tom a new _____ to ride because his old one is broken.

a puppy   **b** coat   **c** bike   **d** bed

Leanne wants to make a special cake for her mom's birthday. She asked her dad, "Will you _____ me?"

a give   **b** help   **c** cook   **d** bake

"Can I have some _____ to eat?" said Daniel, who was hungry.

a cookies   **b** apple   **c** toys   **d** hamburger

Cindy went to her _____ house today, so she did not play with her friends.

a grandmother's   **b** friend's   **c** store   **d** school

CARLOS THE CAR

Fill in the blanks below with the words that make the most sense in each paragraph. Use the the words in each Word Box to help you.

My name is _____. I am a _____. I am just a few years _____. My paint color is_____. My seats are as _____ as the grass. I hold _____ people.

WORD BOX

Carlos	old
green	white
car	two

In the morning my engine is _____ from sitting outside all _____. To start my motor, Carl puts his _____ in the car and turns it on. He steps on the _____. I start to move, but not too quickly. I'm still not quite _____. Soon I can go really _____.

WORD BOX

awake	cold
gas	night
key	fast

Skills: using context clues, drawing conclusions

GETTING THE FACTS

Read each paragraph below. Then answer the questions that follow.

Carolyn's pet is a cat. Her cat lives in her apartment with her. Every day she feeds it cat food. The cat's name is Peaches. Sometimes she plays with the cat.

• Who has a pet cat? _____

• Where does it live? _____

• What does it eat? _____

• Who plays with the cat? _____

Barbara's family has a new car. It is maroon colored. The seats are black. Five people fit in their new car. It has two seat belts in front and three seat belts in the back. They call the car the "Speedy Racer."

• What did the family get? _____

• What color is the car? _____

• How many seat belts are in
  the car? _____

• What color are the seats?

_____

PAMELA'S PARTY

Read the paragraph below. Then answer the questions that follow.

Pamela had a birthday party on Saturday. She had eight friends come to her party at the park. Her mother brought the food and the children brought presents. They had pizza, soft drinks, and a birthday cake with seven candles.

• What kind of party did Pamela have?

_____

• Where was the party?

_____

• How many friends came to her party? _____

• What did they eat? _____

• How old is Pamela? _____

• What is the main idea of this story?_____

_____

• How do you think Pamela felt on Saturday? _____

_____

TOGETHER TIME: Ask an adult to help you plan your own pretend birthday party. Who will come to your party? What food will you serve? What games will you play?

Skills: comprehension, recognizing details, deduction, creativity

THE SMITH FAMILY PICNIC

Read the paragraph below. Then answer the questions that follow.

On Sunday afternoon our whole family is going to the beach to have a picnic. The beach is far from our house, so we have to go there in our car. We need to bring food and some toys to the picnic. There are seven people in my family. We also have several pets—two dogs, a cat, and a turtle. We will stay at the beach all day long.

- What kind of food do you think the family will bring to the picnic? _____
- Which toys will they bring with them? _____ _____
- Which pets will the family take with them on their picnic? _____
- How long will they stay at the beach? _____
- How do you think the family will feel after they return home from the beach? _____

GRADE BOOSTER!

What are your favorite kinds of foods to eat on a picnic at the beach? _____
What are your favorite things to do at the beach?
_____

REVIEW: Comprehension Skills

Read the story below and then answer the questions that follow.

THE CAMPING TRIP

Ken, Dave, and Tom were going on a camping trip to Sequoia National Park with their dad. They packed their car with their camping equipment and food before they went to bed. Early in the morning they left on their trip. They drove for a long time and finally got to the campground. Ken and Dave set up the tent. Tom unrolled all the sleeping bags inside the tent. Their dad went to register at the campsite and found out about all the activities and campfire programs.

- When did they leave to go camping? _____

- Who went to the ranger station to register? _____

- Who set up the tent? _____

- What did Tom do? _____

- Where did they go to camp? _____

- After camp is set up, what do you think they will do?

   _____

- Why do you think they went camping? _____

   _____

Skills: demonstrating mastery of comprehension skills through review

When it comes to
Reading Comprehension

(my name)

IS SUPERB!

CONGRATULATIONS!

_____

(my name)

is a fantastic reader!

Reading
Puzzles & Games

This section offers children opportunities to review the consonants and vowels as well as improve their vocabulary and comprehension skills—all while completing fun puzzles and games. Letter sounds, word recognition and vocabulary, word constuction, and reasoning and comprehension skills are emphasized through this entertaining format.

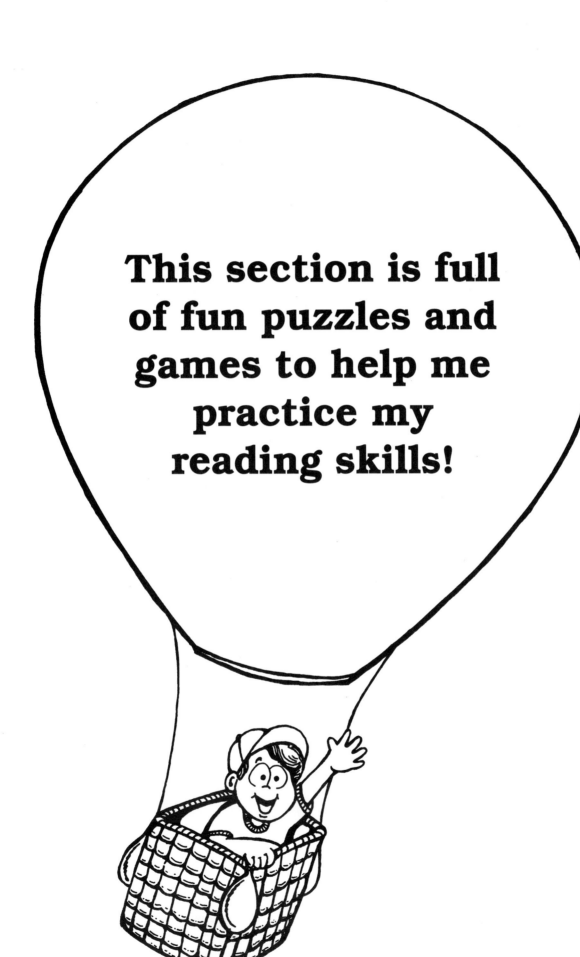

This section is full of fun puzzles and games to help me practice my reading skills!

VOWEL MAZE

Look at the maze below. Find the repeating vowel pattern that will lead you to the end. **Hint:** The first five vowels of the maze make up the repeating pattern.

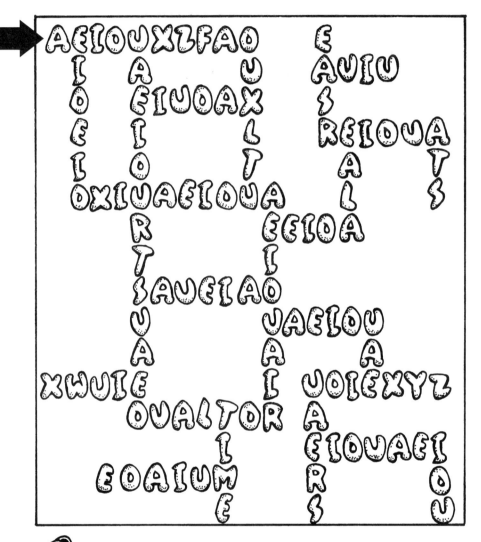

GRADE BOOSTER!

*Can you think of some words that have no vowels in them except for **y**? Make a list of some of these words on a separate piece of paper. Then write a sentence using as many of the words you listed as you can.*

VOWELS IN THE SKY

Follow these instructions to color in the picture below. You will discover something you can find in the sky.

- Color the triangles that contain long vowel words blue.

- Color the triangles that contain short vowel words yellow.

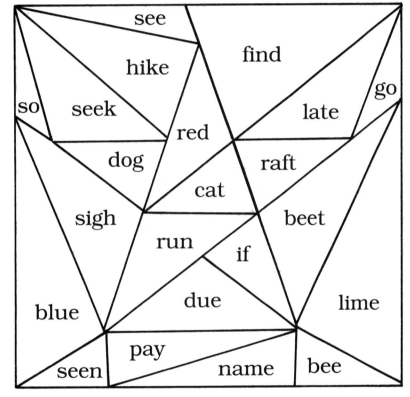

What did you find? A _____

GRADE BOOSTER!

What is astronomy? _____

If you don't know, how can you find out? _____

_____

_____

RECYCLING LETTERS

Dinosaur Bob believes in using everything again and again. This is called **recycling**. Dinosaur Bob even recycles letters. In each of the pairs of words below, one letter from the first word has been used again in the second word. Write the recycled letter on the numbered line next to each pair.

crew   camp $\overline{}$
                   1

camp   outpost $\overline{}$
                   3

bone   old $\overline{}$
                   2

digs   scale $\overline{}$
                   4

Now write the recycled letters on the numbered lines below to answer the riddle.

Which dinosaurs enforced the law in prehistoric times?

tricera $\overline{}$ $\overline{}$ $\overline{}$ $\overline{}$
          1   2   3   4

Skills: letter recognition, identifying patterns, deduction

WHAT COMES NEXT?

Look closely at each row of words below. Then choose a word that should come next. Make sure that the word fits each row's pattern. The words below each blank are clues to help you. There is more than one right answer. **Hint:** If you are not sure what a word means, use a dictionary to find out.

Andy	**B**oris	**C**hris	**D**avid	**E** _____ (NAME)
ant	**e**ggplant	**i**gloo	**o**live	**u** _____ (NOUN)
fairy	**g**remlin	**h**at	**i**ce	**j** _____ (NOUN)
pale	**q**uick	**r**usty	**s**oft	**t** _____ (ADJECTIVE)
swim	**t**wirl	**u**nite	**v**acuum	**w** _____ (VERB)

Skills: letter recognition, identifying patterns, deduction, creativity

JOKING JELLYFISH

Jodie likes to joke with her friends. To answer her riddle, look at the underlined letter in each of the words below. Then unscramble the letters and write the answer in the portholes of the sunken ship.

Skills: recognizing initial letter sounds, deduction, problem solving

ZOO REVIEW

Let's take a trip to the zoo. Look at the animals below. Then write the name of each animal on the sign below that animal's cage. Color all the animals whose names begin with a vowel blue. Color all the animals whose names begin with a consonant red.

Skills: demonstrating mastery of identifying vowels and consonants

CONGRATULATIONS!

This award goes to

_____

(my name)

You are a master of vowels, consonants, and letter recognition!

SYNONYM BAKE SHOP

Synonyms are words that mean the same or close to the same thing. Jen loves baked goodies. But she can only eat cookies that contain pairs of synonyms. Help Jen decide which cookies she can eat by coloring the cookies that contain synonyms brown.

GRADE BOOSTER!

Do you see any cookies that contain pairs of **antonyms**? *Antonyms are words that are opposites. Color the cookies that contain antonyms yellow.*

Skills: identifying synonyms, identifying antonyms, deduction

PREHISTORIC SYNONYMS

Look at the prehistoric animals below. What is each one saying? Can you think of another way to say the same thing? It's easy! Just write a synonym for each underlined word on the line provided.

GRADE BOOSTER!

Write the name of each dinosaur or flying reptile in the picture above. Ask a parent to help you use a dictionary or an encyclopedia if you need help.

Skills: identifying synonyms

ALLIGATOR ANTONYMS

Annie heard this joke from her friends at the swamp: "What kind of alligator do you call when you find ants in your kitchen?"

A $\underline{}$ $\underline{}$ $\underline{}$ $\underline{}$ $\underline{}$ $\underline{}$ $\underline{}$ $\underline{}$ $\underline{}$
  1   2   3   4   5   6   7   8   9

To find the answer, first write in an antonym for each word below. Then write the letter that appears above each number on the numbered lines of the riddle.

near $\underline{}$ $\underline{}$ $\underline{}$
      1

loud $\underline{}$ $\underline{}$ $\underline{}$ $\underline{}$ $\underline{}$ sad $\underline{}$ $\underline{}$ $\underline{}$ $\underline{}$ $\underline{}$
          2   6

big $\underline{}$ $\underline{}$ $\underline{}$ $\underline{}$ $\underline{}$ clean $\underline{}$ $\underline{}$ $\underline{}$ $\underline{}$ $\underline{}$
        3   7

day $\underline{}$ $\underline{}$ $\underline{}$ $\underline{}$ $\underline{}$ cold $\underline{}$ $\underline{}$ $\underline{}$
         4   8

smooth $\underline{}$ $\underline{}$ $\underline{}$ $\underline{}$ $\underline{}$ long $\underline{}$ $\underline{}$ $\underline{}$ $\underline{}$ $\underline{}$
              5   9

DAY AT THE MOTOCROSS RACES

Read the story below and search for the antonyms. Circle each pair of antonyms you find in a different color crayon. The first pair is circled for you.
Hint: You should find five more pairs.

Evan is a (small) boy who rides a (big) bike at the motocross races. He rides with his friends. Some of them are old and some are young. Some go very fast and some go very slow. They all have fun. Evan's bike is new. He likes it better than his old one. The races are usually held during the day, but sometimes they are held at night under the big lights. At the races, Evan's dad shouts, "Go, Evan, go!" At bedtime, his dad whispers, "Good night, Evan, good night."

Skills: identifying antonyms, deduction

RAINING HOMONYMS

Homonyms are words that sound alike but are spelled differently and have different meanings. Write a homonym for each word below in the space provided. When you are finished, write the letter above each number on the numbered lines at the bottom of the page to find the answer to the riddle! Use a dictionary if you need help.

through __ __ __ __ __
     7

see __ __ __
       2

too __ __ __
    1

heard __ __ __ __
     4

wood __ __ __ __ __
     5

slay __ __ __ __ __ __
   3

hoarse __ __ __ __ __
     6

What do you get when you leave a walrus out in the rain?

__ __ __ - __ __ __ __
1 2 3   4 5 6 7

HOMONYM WEB SEARCH

Follow these instructions and color Sidney's spiderweb to find out what he caught in his web.

- Color the shapes that contain homonyms yellow.

- Color the areas that do not contain homonyms green.

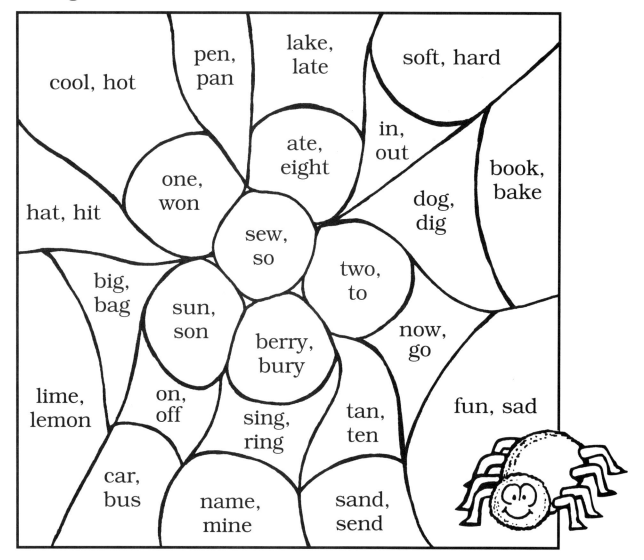

What did Sidney catch in his web? _____

What is a homonym for the object he caught? _____

Skills: identifying homonyms, auditory and visual discrimination, deduction

FOREIGN WORDS

A long, long time ago, people from all over the world went to England and brought their languages with them. The English-speaking people liked many of the words in the languages so much that they made some of them part of the English language. Draw a line from each word below to its meaning and original country.

garage

The class you were in before first grade. This word comes from Germany.

kindergarten

Beans and cheese, or meat, wrapped in a tortilla. This word comes from Mexico.

burrito

The place where a car is put at night. This word comes from France.

TOGETHER TIME: Can you and an adult friend find Germany, Mexico, and France on a map of the world? What foods and other items have Americans borrowed from these countries?

Vocabulary

ENDANGERED ANIMAL TIC-TAC-TOE

Play tic-tac-toe with **endangered animals** from three different **continents**! A continent is a land mass that contains several countries. For example, many of us live in the United States, which is a country on the continent of North America. There are seven continents in the world.

Below are three lists of endangered animals from three different continents. Endangered animals are animals that are close to becoming **extinct,** which means that unless something is done to help them, these animals may not exist anymore. Locate the picture of each animal in the tic-tac-toe grid on the next page. Then write the name of the animal and its home continent on the lines under its picture. One is done for you.

Asia
Indian python
giant panda
orangutan

Africa
African elephant
black rhinoceros
Nile crocodile

Europe
wildcat
loggerhead turtle
barn owl

142   Skills: classification, deduction, vocabulary building, problem solving

Indian python
animal

continent

animal

continent

animal

continent

animal

continent

animal

continent

animal

continent

animal

continent

animal

continent

animal

continent

Which continent has three animals in a row? _____
A row can go across (⟶), down (↓), or diagonally (⟍).

TOGETHER TIME: With an adult friend, think about some reasons why these animals are endangered. Write your answers on a separate piece of paper.

SATURDAY FUN

What do you like to do on Saturdays? Below are some fun things that Martin and Sabrina like to do. Look at the numbered pictures, then look at the crossword puzzle on the next page. Write the name of the activity pictured in the box in the space on the crossword puzzle that has the same number as the picture.

Skills: vocabulary building, deduction, creative thinking, sequencing

What is your favorite thing to do on Saturday?

_____

Which of the activities above could you do if it was a rainy Saturday? _____

_____

Skills: vocabulary building, deduction, creative thinking, sequencing

NEWT THE NUTRITIONIST

Newt the Nutritionist told Anemic Ali and Scurvy Sal that we all need five servings of fruits and vegetables every day to stay healthy! But Ali and Sal can't think of any! Can you help them find the following fruits and vegetables in the word search on the next page?

FRUITS	VEGETABLES
APPLE	ASPARAGUS
APRICOTS	BEETS
BANANA	BROCCOLI
CHERRY	CARROTS
GRAPE	CAULIFLOWER
KIWI	EGGPLANTS
LEMON	LETTUCE
LIME	MUSHROOM
MANGO	ONION
PAPAYA	SNOW PEAS
PEACH	SPINACH
PEAR	SQUASH
STRAWBERRIES	YAMS
WATERMELON	ZUCCHINI

Extra Challenge: Do you know what **anemic** and **scurvy** mean? If not, look them up in the dictionary.

Skills: vocabulary building, visual discrimination

N	U	T	M	U	S	H	R	O	O	M	C	R	I	T	I	O
B	A	N	A	N	A	N	I	S	Q	U	A	S	H	S	T	A
R	A	S	N	L	I	K	E	T	N	C	R	E	W	L	T	P
O	S	H	G	E	L	P	Y	R	O	H	R	U	P	E	A	R
C	P	T	O	O	K	N	O	A	B	E	O	L	I	M	E	I
C	A	U	L	I	F	L	O	W	E	R	T	W	W	O	H	C
O	R	I	P	C	H	F	O	B	E	R	S	K	O	N	D	O
L	A	S	A	P	P	L	E	E	T	Y	K	I	S	P	Y	T
I	G	E	P	E	P	Y	O	R	S	N	O	W	P	E	A	S
U	U	H	A	E	A	L	G	R	A	P	E	I	I	A	M	T
H	S	Y	Y	A	N	O	N	I	O	N	D	F	N	C	S	E
E	L	W	A	T	E	R	M	E	L	O	N	I	A	H	N	G
L	E	T	T	U	C	E	Y	S	O	U	R	B	C	E	S	T
E	G	G	P	L	A	N	T	S	Z	U	C	C	H	I	N	I

Which fruits and vegetables are your favorites? Draw your favorite vegetables on the plate below. Draw your favorite fruits in the fruit bowl below.

LET'S REVIEW

Draw a line from each weather word to the picture it best describes. Then complete each picture by drawing in the correct type of weather in the sky.

SUNNY

RAINY

SNOWY

What is a homonym for **weather**? _____
On a separate sheet of paper, write a sentence using both words.

What is an antonym for **sunny**? _____
Which of these two kinds of weather do you like better? _____

What is a synonym for **cold**? _____
Write a rhyming word for each word: _____

What item do you see in two of the three scenes?

_____
What purpose does it serve in each scene? How are these purposes the same? How are they different? Say your answer out loud.

Skills: rhyming, identifying homonyms, synonyms, antonyms

CONGRATULATIONS!

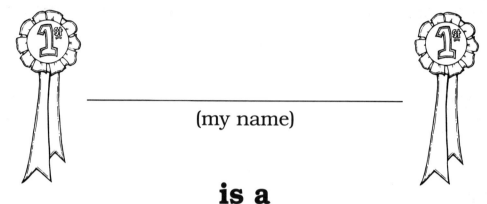

_____

(my name)

is a
champion of synonyms, homonyms,
antonyms, and vocabulary!

MAX AND THE COMPOUND WORD

When two small words are put together to make one bigger word, that bigger word is called a **compound word**. Circle all the compound words in the story below.

Max the mouse loved to sing. He liked it better than baseball or basketball. Almost everyone thought Max had a beautiful voice—everyone except his next-door neighbor. One wintry night Max was in his backyard singing in the moonlight when his neighbor threw a snowball at him. Then he yelled, "Please stop singing, Max. Your voice sounds like a cowbell and it is giving me a toothache! If you come inside, I'll make you some popcorn!" Now, Max liked popcorn even better than singing, so he stopped singing and went inside.

How many compound words did you find? _____

Which of the circled words comes first alphabetically? _____

Which of the circled words comes last alphabetically?_____

GRADE BOOSTER!

On a separate piece of paper, write another story about the adventures of Max the singing mouse. Use at least three compound words in your story.

Skills: identifying compound words, alphabetizing, creativity

COMPOUND CANS

Make tin can telephones by creating compound words.
Draw a string from each can on the left to a can on the
right to connect the words inside the cans. Make sure
the words you form create real compound words.

FUNNY RHYMES

Pepe is playing with rhyming words, and he'd like you to play, too. Read the descriptions he has written below. Then find two rhyming words that mean the same thing as each description. Write the rhyming words on the lines next to each description. Pepe has done the first one for you.

Dollar bills that make
you laugh: <u>*funny money*</u>

What a meowing pet wears
on its head: _____

What a doctor's assistant
carries her wallet in:

_____

A piece of furniture for the fruit that rhymes with **fair**:

_____

What fire plays for fun:_____

What a small rodent wears with slacks: _____

TOGETHER TIME: Ask an adult friend to play a rhyming word game with you. Make up a rhyming pair of words like the ones above. Then describe them to your friend without using the rhyming words. When your friend has guessed your pair, have him or her take a turn and give you a description of a rhyming pair to solve.

Skills: rhyming words, auditory discrimination, deduction, creativity

YAK TRACK

You are about to go on a reading, rhyming adventure through the Himalayas, which is a mountain range in Asia. Are you ready? Be sure to circle all the rhyming words as you go.

You are on the track of a yak who has been known to attack. Since you do not want to lack food on your journey, the pack on your back is very heavy with each yummy snack you brought. As you finally see the yak, you sneak up to it carefully when—crack!—a twig snaps under your feet and the yak turns around. It looks at you and says, "Back, back, you and your pack! You can't track a yak unless you share your snack!"

GRADE BOOSTER!

On a separate piece of paper, write the rhyming words from the story in alphabetical order. If a word appears more than once in the story, you only need to write it one time.

PLURAL POWER

Plural words are words that mean more than one. You can make most nouns plural by adding **s** to the end of the word. Write the plural form of each word on the line next to the picture.

chick _____

book _____

lizard _____

Some words change forms when they become plural. These words are called **irregular plurals**. Write each irregular plural on the line provided. Then draw a picture of each word in the box next to its plural.

mouse _____

tooth _____

leaf _____

Skills: writing plural word forms, creativity

FISHING FOR CONTRACTIONS

A **contraction** is a word that stands for two words. Circle the five contractions in the story below.

Michele and Evan weren't in school during the summer. They had a lot of time on their hands. One day Evan said, "Let's go fishing." The two of them took a boat out on the river. Michele wouldn't fish, but she said, "I'm going to tell jokes while you fish." After a while, Evan couldn't fish anymore—he was laughing too hard.

Write the five contractions in alphabetical order on the lines below. Then use the numbered spaces to find the answer to one of Michele's jokes.

$$\frac{\quad}{\,} \; \frac{\quad}{5} \; \frac{\quad}{\,} \; \frac{\quad}{\,} \; \frac{\quad}{\,} \; \frac{\quad}{\,} \, ' \, \frac{\quad}{1}$$

$$\frac{\quad}{\,} \, ' \, \frac{\quad}{7}$$

$$\frac{\quad}{\,} \; \frac{\quad}{\,} \; \frac{\quad}{\,} \, ' \, \frac{\quad}{8}$$

$$\frac{\quad}{2} \; \frac{\quad}{\,} \; \frac{\quad}{6} \; \frac{\quad}{\,} \; \frac{\quad}{\,} \, ' \, \frac{\quad}{\,}$$

$$\frac{\quad}{4} \; \frac{\quad}{3} \; \frac{\quad}{\,} \; \frac{\quad}{\,} \; \frac{\quad}{\,} \; \frac{\quad}{\,} \, ' \, \frac{\quad}{\,}$$

Why wasn't there much fishing on Noah's Ark?

There were only $\dfrac{\quad}{1} \; \dfrac{\quad}{2} \; \dfrac{\quad}{3} \qquad \dfrac{\quad}{4} \; \dfrac{\quad}{5} \; \dfrac{\quad}{6} \; \dfrac{\quad}{7} \; \dfrac{\quad}{8}$.

CONTRACTION CODES

Detective Dan needs your help to crack the case of the contractions! Use the code breaker on the next page to help you fill in the correct contractions below. Then write the two words that each contraction stands for next to or below it. Dan has done the first one to get you started.

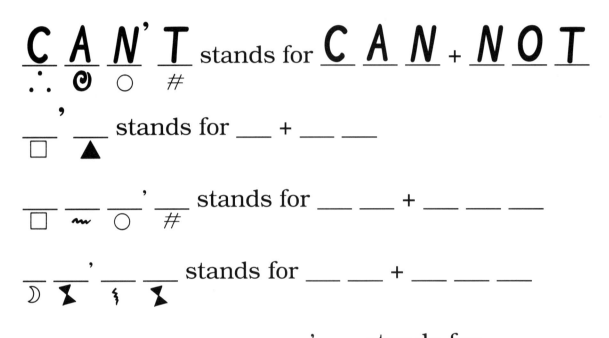

Skills: identifying contractions, decoding, visual discrimination

CODE BREAKER

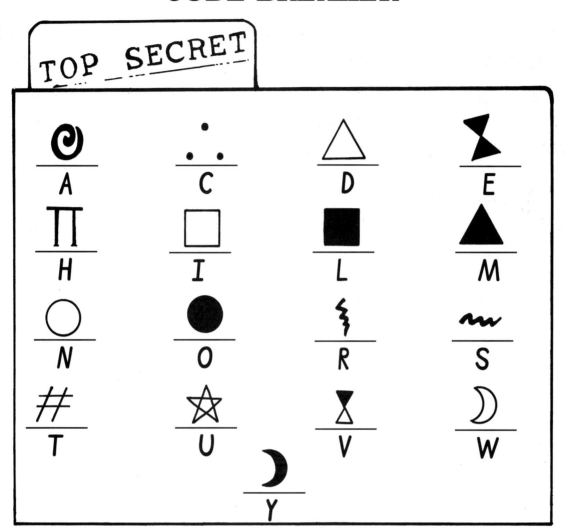

GRADE BOOSTER!

The symbols Δ and Π in the code above are real letters from an alphabet that is printed below. What language is that alphabet used in? In what country do they speak that language? If you do not know, how could you find out? Look closely at the alphabet below. Do you recognize any letters from the alphabet used in the English language?

ΑΒΓΔΕΖΧΦΗΙΚΛΜΝΞΟΠΘΡΣΤΥΩΨ

SYLLABLE PYRAMID

Amir lives in the desert in Egypt. Today, Amir is taking you to a special syllable pyramid. Each of its blocks has a one-, two-, or three-syllable word. Color the blocks with two-syllable words red. Color the blocks with three-syllable words brown. Read the words on the uncolored blocks to answer the question below.

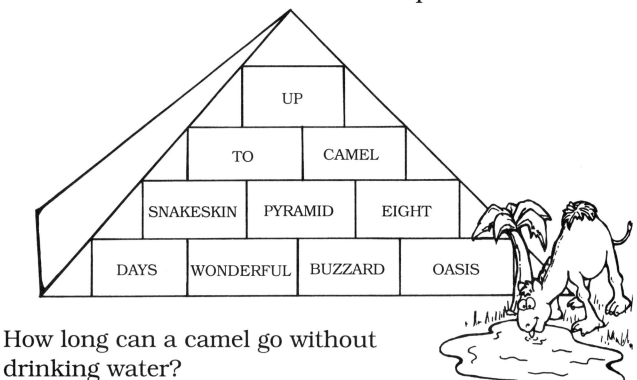

How long can a camel go without drinking water?

_____

GRADE BOOSTER!

Which of the words in the pyramid is a compound word? _____

What two words is it made up of?

_____ + _____

BIRTHDAY FEAST

The three friends below are at a birthday party. Look at the foods that are served there. Then read the clues and draw a line from each food item to the friend who will eat it. Remember, some food items may be eaten by more than one friend.

• Slim Suzy only eats foods with one syllable.

• Finicky Fred only eats foods that begin and end with the same letter.

• Omnivorous Oliver eats all the other foods that Fred and Suzy don't eat.

GRADE BOOSTER!

Which friend gets to eat the most foods at the party? _____ Who eats the least? _____ Can you think of some other types of foods that each friend can eat? List them on a separate piece of paper.

HORSE SHOW REVIEW

Mary Lou is showing her horse, Magellan, in a horse show. As she walks around the show ring, many people say nice things about Magellan. Look at what they say, then follow the directions.

- Put a rectangle around the word that has three syllables.
- Circle the plural word.
- Underline the contraction.
- Draw a line connecting the two words that rhyme.

Skills: syllabication, plurals, contractions, rhyming, following directions

Celebrate!

_____

(my name)

is an independent reader!

OCEAN ODDITIES

Carleton the scuba diver is taking you on an undersea journey! Do you notice anything that seems out of place in the ocean? Things that are strange or do not belong are called **oddities**. Circle the oddities you see in the ocean.

GRADE BOOSTER!

What is the first letter of each ocean oddity that you circled? Together these letters spell a word. Unscramble the letters to see what Carleton hopes to find in the ocean: _____

Skills: classification, problem solving, visual discrimination

FOREST FUN

John is going on a hike through the forest. Complete the picture by drawing in some of the things he might see on his hike. When you are done, make a list of the items you drew on the lines provided.

FOREST FINDINGS

_____

_____

_____

_____

_____

_____

_____

_____

WHAT COMES NEXT?

Look closely at the pairs in each row. Then write the word or draw the picture that comes next on the line provided. There is only one right answer for each.

lime: green   tomato: red   lemon: _____

cucumber: pickle   plum: prune   grape: _____

The pairs of words in the row below also follow a pattern. Look at each pair. Then choose a word to fill in the blank. There may be more than one right answer.

flour: cake   cotton: shirt   wood: _____

TOGETHER TIME: Take a trip to the library with an adult to find the answers to the following questions: How does a cucumber become a pickle? How does a grape become a raisin? How are these processes different? How are they the same?

Skills: analogies, classification, pattern recognition, deduction, creativity

PICTURE WORDS

At a construction site, you can see many things. To find out what you might see, decode the puzzles below. Write the word for each picture on the lines provided. Then subtract or add the letters as directed. Put together the leftover letters to get your answer. The first one has been done for you.

(harp) - rp + (swimmer) - swi =

<u>HARP</u> - rp + <u>SWIMMER</u> - swi = <u>HAMMER</u>

(witch) - itch + (moon) - mn + (dog) - og =

_____ - itch + _____ - mn + _____ - og = _____

(crown) - own + (fan) - f + (egg) - gg =

_____ - own + _____ - f + _____ - gg = _____

(worm) - m + (kite) - ite + (cat) - cal

_____ - m + _____ - ite + _____ - cal

+ (nest) - est =

+ _____ - est = _____

Which word is a compound word? Circle it. Which word has a long vowel sound? Put a star next to it.

THE BIG CATS

A **fact** is something that can be proven as true. An **opinion** is a person's belief or feeling. Read the story below and then follow the directions on the next page.

Amy takes tour groups on safaris in Africa. Amy's favorite animals on the safaris are the big cats, which include cheetahs, leopards, and lions. Cheetahs can run 80 miles per hour. The leopard is not as fast as the cheetah, but it is more savage. The leopard can climb trees and leap onto its prey. Also, the leopard is prettier than the cheetah.

Many people on Amy's safari tours ask to see the tigers, which are also big cats. Lots of people think tigers live in Africa. Amy tells them that they need to go to India to see tigers. Tigers don't live in Africa.

Amy likes to point out groups of lions, called a **pride,** sleeping in the shade. She tells her tour groups that the lion is a more gentle cat than the cheetah and the leopard.

Skills: identifying fact vs. opinion, reading comprehension, visual discrimination

Write two facts from the story:

_____

_____

_____

_____

_____

Write two opinions from the story:

_____

_____

_____

_____

_____

Cross out the letters **C, A, T,** and **S** in this string of letters to find the answer to the question below.

C A T M O T S R N C A T I N T S G

During what part of the day do lions like to hunt?

_____

CAUSE AND EFFECT PAIRS

A **cause** is an action, or act, that makes something happen. An **effect** is something that happens because of an action or a cause.

Look at the sentences below. Draw a line from each cause on the left to its effect on the right.

Jessica did not sleep well last night.

Eric was very happy.

Dante always shared his toys.

Jessica is tired.

Melissa ate three pieces of pie.

Melissa felt sick.

Eric was on vacation from school.

Everyone wanted to play with Dante.

Skills: identifying cause and effect, reasoning, deduction

OCEAN KAYAKING WITH OLAF

Read the story, then fill in the blanks below.

One day, Olaf went kayaking. He launched himself out into the open ocean. There he saw a beautiful whale. Olaf had no fear of this gentle giant. He paddled his kayak through the water toward it. He leaned over the side of his kayak to try to touch the whale's back. But he leaned too far and—splash—he fell into the water. The whale seemed happy to have a playmate and allowed Olaf to grab on to its fin and go for a ride. Together Olaf and the whale swam through the waters, greeting otters, dolphins, and other ocean dwellers. Then the whale decided he wanted to dive down deep into the ocean, so Olaf let go and swam back to his waiting kayak.

CAUSE	EFFECT
Olaf had no fear of the whale.	_____
_____	Olaf's kayak moved through the water.
Olaf leaned over too far in his kayak.	_____
_____	Olaf let go of the whale's fin.

A SNOWY REVIEW

1. Draw a line from the statement on the left to each word or picture it describes on the right.

ski

These are things David and his friends can do in the snow.

snowboard

swim

2. Look at what David and his friends are saying below. Then write **fact** or **opinion** under what each of them says.

"Making snow people is fun!"

"No two snowflakes are exactly alike."

"Sledding is my favorite sport!"

_____ _____ _____

3. On a separate piece of paper, write your own story about a day in the snow with your friends. Use three cause and effect relationships in your story.

You're Really Cooking Now!

_____
(my name)

is
boiling over with
reasoning skills!

JOURNEY INTO SPACE

Complete the story of Colin's trip into space. Fill in each blank with one of the words that is floating in space. The other words in the sentence, called the **context,** will help you figure out which word fits best.

Colin flew to the moon in a _____. Colin brought Bruno, his pet _____, with him into space. When they looked out the _____, they saw lots of stars. When Bruno got _____, Colin gave him some space snacks. When Colin and Bruno became sleepy, they went to _____.

window

bed

bananas

monkey

hungry

fuel

spaceship

What do spaceships use for power? _____

Hint: Look at the leftover words to find the answer to the question.

GRADE BOOSTER!

Would you like to go on a trip into space? On a separate piece of paper, write three things you would bring with you on your journey. The things can be objects, people, or pets. Then tell why you want to bring these things.

172

FINISH THE STORY

Fill in the blanks to complete the story below. You can use words, pictures, or both to fill in the blanks. You will need to fill in some blanks with more than one word. Choose your own words and pictures, or use some of the words in the box below.

There was an ☺ who lived in a 🏠 by the 〰️ .

She lived there with her 🐕 . The 🐕 had _____ fur and only barked when _____ .

The 👵 took her 🐕 for a walk along the 〰️ .

There they saw a _____ come out of the 🌊 and smile at them. Then the _____ took

a big breath and said, "_____."

The old lady said, " _____," and her

🐕 _____ .

stars	Good-bye	bicycle	green
bring	heard	whale	noises
Thank you	love	pony	sneezed
	pine needles	whale	
	whispering		

Skills: using context clues, reasoning, deduction, creativity

TRACK STAR

Number each picture in the boxes below to tell the story in order.

Michele lined up
at the starting line.

Michele put on her
track shoes.

Michele won
first place!

Michele stretched
her muscles.

Michele ran
the race.

Skills: sequencing, comprehension, reasoning

A PIGLET'S TALE

Number the sentences below to tell the story in order.

___ Then he was a happy piglet.

___ His friends all said, "You eat a lot."

___ Then one day he read that piglets are supposed to eat a lot.

___ He worried about what his friends said.

___ Once there was a piglet, which is a baby pig.

Draw a picture to illustrate the story of piglet.

WATERMELON CONTEST

Read the story and then follow the directions below.

Laurie and Chip went to the county fair. They entered a watermelon-eating contest. Watermelon is Laurie's favorite food. They had to eat an entire watermelon with no hands. For Laurie, it was no problem. She ate the watermelon very quickly. She won the contest. Laurie's face was very sticky, but she was very satisfied.

Circle the slice that shows the main idea of the story:

Laurie likes watermelon more than any other food.

Laurie was sticky from head to toe.

Laurie entered a watermelon-eating contest and won.

Laurie likes going to county fairs with Chip in the summer.

GRADE BOOSTER!

*How many words can you spell using the letters in **watermelon**? Write the words on the lines below.*
WATERMELON

_____   _____   _____

_____   _____   _____

_____   _____   _____

Skills: finding the main idea, comprehension, deduction, creativity

GIOVANNI PLAYS SOCCER

Read the short story below, then circle the picture that illustrates the story.

Giovanni is going to play soccer. He is wearing his new soccer shorts. His dad is going to drive him to the soccer field.

Circle the item in the other pictures that does not match the story.

Skills: comprehension, deduction, reasoning

GUS THE GOAT

Read the story below, then answer the questions.

Gus the goat is always hungry. One morning Gus woke up feeling especially hungry. He got out of bed, stretched, and then went in search of food. Food for Gus is not like food for you and me. Gus eats all kinds of objects. Gus went out his front gate and ate a flower. Then he crossed the street and devoured his neighbor's mailbox—mail and all! But he was still hungry, so he went to the library and swallowed three copies of the book *Moby Dick*. Feeling smarter, but still not full, he left the library and went to the antique shop. There Gus ate an antique chest of drawers, which finally filled him up!

Circle the items below that were part of Gus's meal.

Which item did Gus eat first? Put a square around that item. Which item did Gus eat last? Put a triangle around that item.

Skills: comprehension, sequencing, recall

FINISH THE HOUSE

Read the story below, then use crayons to complete the picture to match the story.

Sandra is an architect—someone who designs buildings. Sandra is building her dream house. It has a large red front door, a chimney, a porch swing, yellow curtains, and a wishing well in the front yard.

GRADE BOOSTER!

If Sandra lit a fire in her fireplace, what would you add to the picture to show this?

_____

Skills: comprehension, recognizing details, creativity   **179**

AIRPLANE SEARCH

Read the story below, then follow the directions.

Stuart and Veronica went on vacation with their parents. They went to the beach. The beach is far away from their house, so they flew there in an airplane. The airplane they flew in was red. It had three blue stripes on each wing, a dot on the tail, and two pilots in the cockpit.

Color the airplane that Stuart and Veronica flew in.

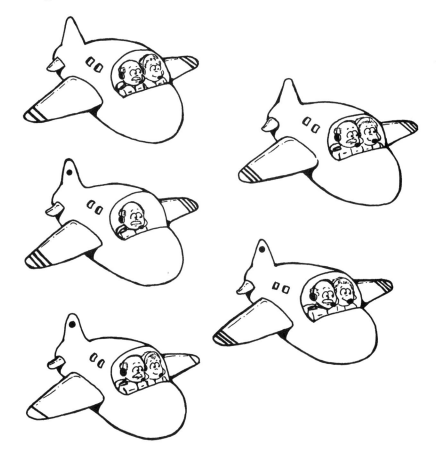

TOGETHER TIME: With an adult friend, plan a pretend trip to any place in the world. Decide where you will go, what you will bring, how long you will stay, and what activities you and your adult friend will do there.

Skills: comprehension, deduction, visual discrimination, creativity

GRETA THE GHOST BAT

Read the story below, then answer the questions.

In Australia, there once lived a ghost bat named Greta. Ghost bats get their name because their beautiful pale fur looks like it glows in the moonlight. Greta lived with her father. Each night, they soared over deserts and forests in search of insects for dinner. By day, they slept in an old, dark gold-mining shaft. One day, Greta woke as the sun was going down to find that her father was gone. Using her echolocation, a bat's way of seeing in the dark, Greta flew around the mine looking for her father. Suddenly, she heard a loud "Surprise!" Her father had gathered all of Greta's ghost bat friends together to give her a surprise birthday party!

In what part of the world does Greta live? _____

What do you think Greta is usually doing at noon?

_____

How do you think Greta felt when she woke to find her father gone? _____

Congratulations

_____
(my name)

**has a ticket on the
Air Super Reader Express!
You're flying high!**

Math

This section builds fundamental math skills using critical and creative thinking. The clever exercises include counting and estimating, addition, subtraction, multiplication, an introduction to division through fractions, as well as interpreting clues, organizing data, and reaching conclusions through reasoning.

I know my numbers
and how to count,
and now I am
beginning to add,
subtract, and multiply!

MY NEW MATH WORDS: About Adding

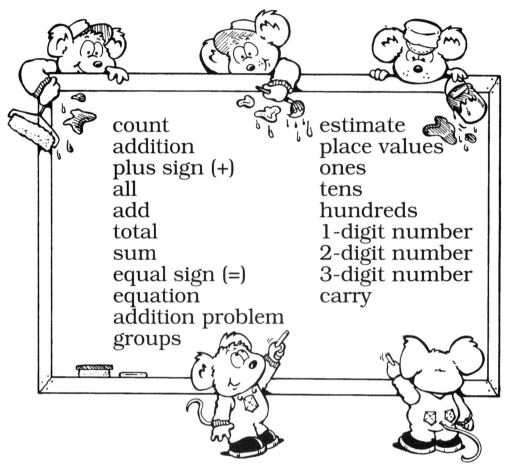

count
addition
plus sign (+)
all
add
total
sum
equal sign (=)
equation
addition problem
groups

estimate
place values
ones
tens
hundreds
1-digit number
2-digit number
3-digit number
carry

These are math words that you learn in second grade. Have you seen any of them before? Circle the words that you have seen before.

Below are math words or phrases you use all the time! Draw a line from each math word or phrase to the picture it describes.

telephone number   address   age   zip code   weight

Skills: math literacy, associating numbers with life, identifying words to solve problems

By now you are a great counter. So let's practice **counting** by twos. When you **count** by twos, you skip every other number. Start with the number 2 and **count** all the way to 100. Say each number out loud as you **count**. Be sure to fill in any numbers that are missing from the chart.

2, 4, 6, 8 . . . I can count by twos!

2	4		8	10
	14	16		20
22				30
	34	36	38	
		46	48	
52	54			60
62				70
	74	76		
	84		88	90
		96		

GRADE BOOSTER!

What do all the numbers above have in common?

_____

Now let's practice counting by fives. But this time instead of writing the numerals, you are going to *spell* them. Fill in the lines below by writing the numbers as words as you count by fives. When you are done, say each number out loud.

TEN

5   five

10   ten

15   fifteen

20   twenty

25   twenty-five

30   thirty

35   thirty-five

40   forty

45   forty-five

50   fifty

TOGETHER TIME: Can you spell all the numbers from 1 to 50 as words? Ask your mom, dad, or a friend to help you spell each number on a separate piece of paper. Be sure to write them in the proper numerical order.

    Skills: number recognition, counting by fives, writing words for numbers: 1–50

A **digit** is a whole number. The numbers 0 1 2 3 4 5 6 7 8 9 are **1-digit numbers**. They are made up of only 1 number.

Numbers between 10 and 99 are **2-digit numbers**. The numbers 10 15 21 35 46 57 66 79 81 98 are **2-digit numbers**. They are made up of 2 numbers.

Numbers between 100 and 999 are called **3-digit numbers**. The numbers 110 224 346 450 465 575 687 798 800 901 are all **3-digit numbers**. They are made up of 3 numbers.

Let's practice identifying **1-digit, 2-digit,** and **3-digit numbers**. Circle the correct number of digits in each box. The first one is done for you.

24	7	35
1 ② 3	1 2 3	1 2 3
101	51	6
1 2 3	1 2 3	1 2 3
8	49	120
1 2 3	1 2 3	1 2 3

Place Values

Now that you are a whiz at counting 1-digit, 2-digit, and 3-digit numbers, let's learn about **place values**. Look at the number 10. It has two digits: 1 and 0. This means it has two **place values**.

The 0 on the right side is in the **ones' place value**.

10

The 1 on the left is in the **tens' place value**.

Frieda and Freddy write their tens' digit and ones' digit in boxes like this:

tens	ones
1	0

To write the number 12, Freddy writes the number 1 in the **tens' place**. Frieda writes the number 2 in the **ones' place**.

tens	ones
1	2

This makes the 2-digit number 12.

tens	ones
1	2

Skills: place values for tens and ones

Now it's your turn to separate some 2-digit numbers into their correct place values.

85
tens	ones

32
tens	ones

64
tens	ones

71
tens	ones

90
tens	ones

45
tens	ones

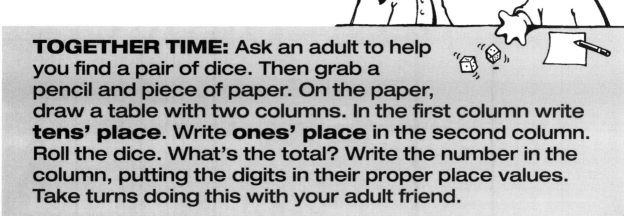

TOGETHER TIME: Ask an adult to help you find a pair of dice. Then grab a pencil and piece of paper. On the paper, draw a table with two columns. In the first column write **tens' place**. Write **ones' place** in the second column. Roll the dice. What's the total? Write the number in the column, putting the digits in their proper place values. Take turns doing this with your adult friend.

Estimation

Sometimes there are so many items in a group that it would take a *really* long time to count them all. How can you find out how many items there are? You can **estimate**, or guess.

Let's practice. Look at the picture below and estimate how many pieces of candy are in the bag. Are there more than 10 pieces? Are there less than 20? Write your estimate in the space provided. Then count the pieces of candy. Was your estimate more, less, or exactly the same as the actual number?

I AM NOT SURE HOW MANY PIECES THERE ARE. WHAT DO YOU THINK?

My estimate: _____

Actual number of pieces: _____

TOGETHER TIME: Ask your mom, dad, or a friend to help you gather some coins. Place the coins on a table. **Estimate** how many coins there are. Write your guess on a separate piece of paper. Ask your mom, dad, or friend to make an **estimate**. Write down his or her guess. Then count the coins. How many are there? Was your **estimate** more, less, or exactly the same as the actual number? What about your mom's, dad's, or friend's guess? Whose **estimate** was closer to the actual number?

Skills: estimating, distinguishing amounts in groups

You have 20 friends coming to your birthday party.
You want to make sure that there is enough food for
each one of your guests to have 1 of each item. First
estimate how much food is in each group. Then count
the actual number in those groups.

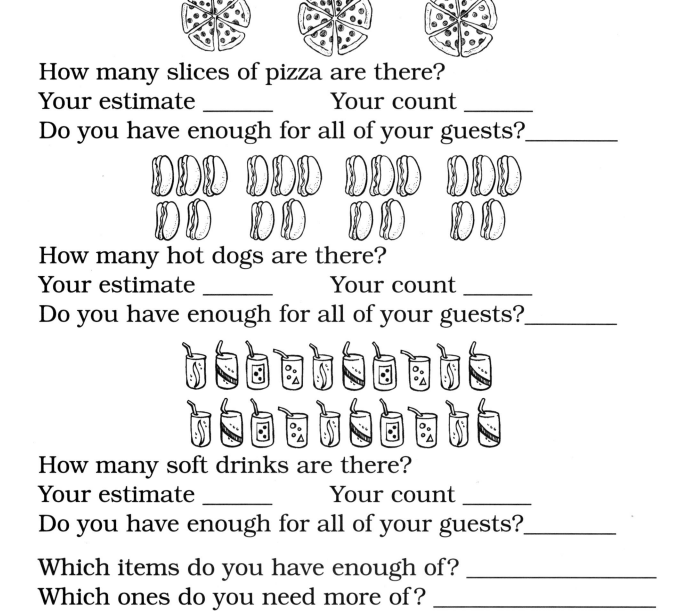

How many slices of pizza are there?

Your estimate _____   Your count _____

Do you have enough for all of your guests?_____

How many hot dogs are there?

Your estimate _____   Your count _____

Do you have enough for all of your guests?_____

How many soft drinks are there?

Your estimate _____   Your count _____

Do you have enough for all of your guests?_____

Which items do you have enough of? _____

Which ones do you need more of ? _____

How much more do you need? _____

Look at these pictures. How many items do you think are in each group? How many do you think there are in all? Write each estimate in the spaces provided. Then count the items. Was your estimate more, less, or exactly the same as the actual number?

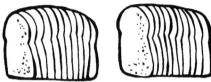

How many bread slices are there?

Your estimate:	**Actual:**
in each loaf: _____	in each loaf: _____
in all: _____	in all: _____

How many eggs are there?

Your estimate:	**Actual:**
in each carton: _____	in each carton: _____
in all: _____	in all: _____

How many pieces of popcorn are there?

Your estimate:	**Actual:**
in each pot: _____	in each pot: _____
in all: _____	in all: _____

Skills: estimating, distinguishing amounts in groups

Putting numbers together is called **addition**. The picture symbol used for addition is called a **plus sign (+)**. Look at the pictures below. Then answer the questions using addition.

Three clowns are riding.   Two more want to join them.

How many clowns are riding bikes? _____
How many more clowns have come to ride? _____
How many clowns are there **in all**? **Add** them: _____

When you add two numbers together, you get a **total**, or a **sum**. This is sometimes referred to as **in all**. The picture symbol used for a total is an **equal sign (=)**.

Look at this addition problem:

3 🤡 s + 2 🤡 s = 5 🤡 s

3 clowns riding bikes plus 2 more equals 5 clowns in all.

1   2   3   4   5

Bertha practices adding her 2s, 3s, and 4s in addition flowers. Can you help her fill in the answers for each problem? A few are done for you.

GRADE BOOSTER!

Solve this problem and write the sum. Then make up a story problem that tells about this addition problem. Give it to a friend or a family member to solve. Did that person get the same answer as you?

8 🍐s + 4 🍐s = _____

Now it's time to learn **2-digit addition**. Take a look at the rules below.

How to add **2-digit numbers:**
1. **Add the numbers in the ones' place.**
2. **If there are more than 10 ones, carry to the tens' place.**
3. **Add the numbers in the tens' place.**
4. **Write the sum, or total.**

Let's practice by adding these numbers.

$$\begin{array}{r} 12 \\ +\ 2 \\ \end{array}$$

12 carrots   **+**   **2 carrots = _____**

First add the numbers in the ones' place.
Are there more than 10 ones? ____ yes __X__ no.

$$\begin{array}{r} 12 \\ +\ 2 \\ \end{array}$$ (Think: 2 + 2 = 4)

Write the number of ones.   **4**
Now add the numbers in the tens' place.

(Think: 1 + 0 = 1)
$$\begin{array}{r} 12 \\ +\ 02 \\ \hline 14 \end{array}$$

Write the number of tens.   **14**
The sum, or total, equals 14.

2-Digit Addition

When you add numbers in the ones' place and your total is a 2-digit number, you need to **carry**. Write the ones in the ones' column. Then carry over the tens to the tens' column and add the numbers in the tens' column together.

Rudy has 16 ears of corn. He finds 5 more. How many ears of corn does he have in all?

$+$ $=$ _____   or $\begin{array}{r} 16 \\ + 5 \\ \hline \end{array}$

First add the numbers in the ones' place.
Are there more than 10 ones? __X__ yes ____ no

$\begin{array}{r} {}^{1}16 \\ + 5 \\ \hline 1 \end{array}$ ⌐11 Think: 6 + 5 = 11

6 plus 5 equals 11. There are 11 ones. So we need to **carry**. Write the ones in the ones' place. **Carry** the tens to the tens' place.

Now add the numbers in the tens' place.

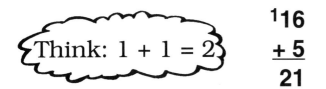

Think: 1 + 1 = 2 $\begin{array}{r} {}^{1}16 \\ + 5 \\ \hline 21 \end{array}$

The sum, or total, equals _____.

         Skills: 2-digit addition, carrying tens

yes? no?

Ollie is adding 3 shells to the 19 shells that he already has. Circle **yes** if he should carry tens. Circle **no** if he shouldn't, then solve the problem.

```
  19
+  3
```

Look at these problems. Do you need to carry? Check "yes" or "no," then help Ollie solve each problem.

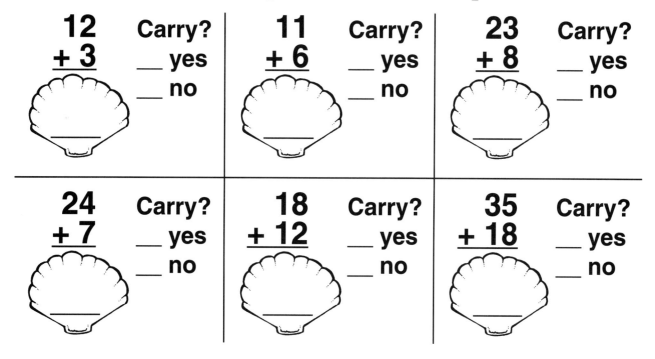

```
  12      Carry?
+  3      __ yes
          __ no
```

```
  11      Carry?
+  6      __ yes
          __ no
```

```
  23      Carry?
+  8      __ yes
          __ no
```

```
  24      Carry?
+  7      __ yes
          __ no
```

```
  18      Carry?
+ 12      __ yes
          __ no
```

```
  35      Carry?
+ 18      __ yes
          __ no
```

TOGETHER TIME: Ask an adult to make up six challenging 2-digit addition problems for you to solve. Be sure that at least four of those problems involve carrying.

Skills: 1- and 2-digit addition, carrying tens

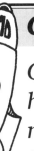

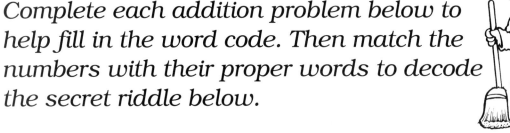

GRADE BOOSTER!

Complete each addition problem below to help fill in the word code. Then match the numbers with their proper words to decode the secret riddle below.

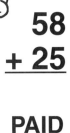

58 + 25	22 + 12	12 + 13	30 + 17
PAID	WHO	DAY'S	GETS
12 + 17	37 + 15	60 + 32	10 + 10
JOB	NEVER	JANITOR	FULL
55 + 13	11 + 10	43 + 18	35 + 24
A	FOR	NIGHT	THE

_____ _____ _____ _____
34   52   47   83

_____ _____ _____ _____ _____?
21   68   20   25   29

_____ _____ _____
68   61   92

Now it's time to learn about the **hundreds' place value**. Look at the number 132. It has three digits: 1, 3, and 2. This means it takes up three **place values**.

The 1 on the left side is in the **hundreds' place value**.

132

The 2 on the right side is in the **ones' place value**.

The 3 in the center is in the **tens' place value**.

Charlie writes his hundreds, tens, and ones in boxes like this:

hundreds	tens	ones
1	3	2

To write the number 124, Charlie writes the number 1 in the **hundreds' place**.

hundreds
1

Charlie writes the number 2 in the **tens' place**.

tens
2

Then Charlie writes the number 4 in the **ones' place**.

ones
4

When he's finished, he has the 3-digit number 124!

How to add **3-digit numbers:**

1. Add the numbers in the ones' place.
2. If there are more than 10 ones, carry to the tens' place.
3. Add the numbers in the tens' place.
4. If there are more than 10 tens, carry to the hundreds' place.
5. Write the sum, or total.

Let's practice adding 3-digit numbers without carrying.

Add the numbers in the ones' place.

$$\begin{array}{r} 2\,4\,1 \\ +\,1\,3\,8 \\ \hline 9 \end{array}\;9$$

1 plus 8 equals 9.

Add the numbers in the tens' place.

$$\begin{array}{r} 2\,4\,1 \\ +\,1\,3\,8 \\ \hline 7\,9 \end{array}\;7$$

4 plus 3 equals 7.

Add the numbers in the hundreds' place.

$$3\begin{array}{r} 2\,4\,1 \\ +\,1\,3\,8 \\ \hline 3\,7\,9 \end{array}$$

2 plus 1 equals 3.

The answer is the sum, or total.

Now let's see how to **carry** ones and tens in 3-digit addition.

First add the ones' place.

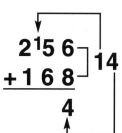

6 plus 8 equals 14. Carry 1 ten for 10 ones. Now you have 4 ones left.

Then add the tens' place.

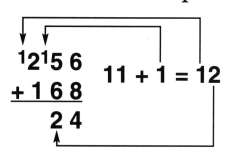

$$11 + 1 = 12$$

5 plus 6 equals 11. Add the 1 ten you carried over to the tens' place. 11 plus 1 equals 12 tens. You have more than 10 tens. Carry 10 tens (which is 1 hundred) to the hundreds' place. You have 2 tens left.

Next add the hundreds' place.

$$3 + 1 = 4$$

```
 ¹2¹5 6
+  1 6 8
  4 2 4
```

2 hundred plus 1 hundred equals 3 hundred. Add the 1 hundred you carried over. Now you have 4 hundreds.

The answer is the sum, or total.

3-Digit Addition

Use addition to find out how much Paul and Patty weigh altogether.

Paul weighs 165 pounds.

Patty weighs 158 pounds.

Can you write an **equation** to show how much the pandas weigh? An **equation** is a math sentence using symbols.

Think: +
(Paul's weight)
(Patty's weight)
(total weight)

_____ + _____ = _____
(Paul's weight)   (Patty's weight)   (total weight)

Did you carry any tens? ___ yes ___ no
Did you carry any hundreds? ___ yes ___ no

Skills: 3-digit addition, carrying tens and ones, writing addition equations

Paul and Patty are hungry. Help them find the shortest path to the sugar cane field to have lunch. Look at the map below. Which path looks the shortest? A, B, or C? Take a guess. Do you remember what this kind of guess is called? It's an **estimate**.

Write your estimate here: _____

Now add the number of miles in each path to find the shortest way. Use another piece of paper if you need more room to solve these 3-digit addition problems. Then write your answer below.

PANDAVILLE MAP

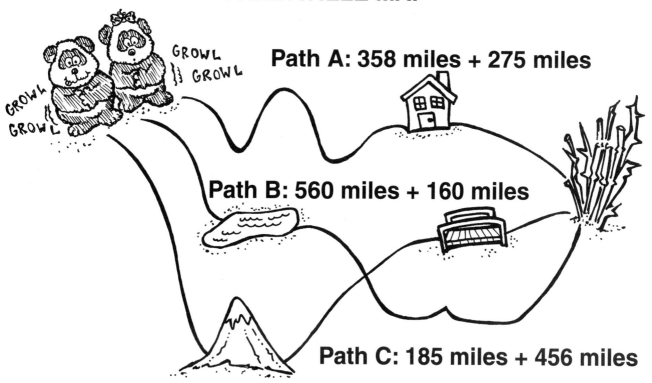

Path A: 358 miles + 275 miles

Path B: 560 miles + 160 miles

Path C: 185 miles + 456 miles

When you add the miles of each path, you find out that the shortest path is Path _____.

The monkey triplets do everything together. Now they are going to add some 3-digit numbers together. Help them by following the steps for adding 3-digit numbers on page 204. The first one is done for you.

```
  2 3 8        3 7 1
+ 4 8 7      + 2 4 3
-------
  7 2 5
```

```
  6 2 1        9 6 3
+ 3 8 3      + 1 7 4
```

GRADE BOOSTER!

Are you ready to test your knowledge? Solve this 3-digit addition problem. Then add your sum to 779. What is your total?

$635 + 367 = $ _____

_____ $+ 779 = $ _____

Skills: 3-digit addition problems, carrying tens and ones

Each monster needs to find its proper number for the race. Complete the addition problems below to figure out which monster gets which number. Then write the correct numbers on the monsters' shirts.

$$\begin{array}{r} 132 \\ + 121 \\ \hline \end{array}$$

$$\begin{array}{r} 198 \\ + 124 \\ \hline \end{array}$$

$$\begin{array}{r} 345 \\ + 101 \\ \hline \end{array}$$

$$\begin{array}{r} 497 \\ + 173 \\ \hline \end{array}$$

$$\begin{array}{r} 415 \\ + 307 \\ \hline \end{array}$$

Skills: 3-digit addition with carrying

LET'S REVIEW: ADDITION

Write the total number of triangles.

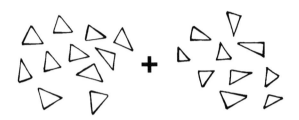

How many animal cookies are there in all?

Total: _____

_____ + _____ = _____

___

Add these 2-digit numbers.

$$\begin{array}{r} 3\,8 \\ +\,3\,8 \\ \hline \end{array}$$

Add these 3-digit numbers.

$$\begin{array}{r} 4\,5\,9 \\ +\,3\,4\,5 \\ \hline \end{array}$$

Do you have to carry the ones?

Check one: ___ yes ___ no

Skills: 1-, 2-, and 3-digit addition with carrying, writing equations

Award Certificate

_____
(my name)

Is One Super Addition Mathematician

Add each problem to fill in the letter code. Then match the numbers with their proper letters to decode the secret message below.

4 + 6 = ___ A   9 + 9 = ___ B   7 + 7 = ___ C   400 + 200 = ___ D

15 + 3 = ___ E   14 + 2 = ___ F   15 + 5 = ___ G   14 + 7 = ___ H

120 + 10 = ___ I   16 + 1 = ___ J   30 + 18 = ___ K

100 + 20 = ___ L   117 + 14 = ___ M   4 + 3 = ___ N   42 + 8 = ___ O

130 ___ '131 ___   14 ___   50 ___   50 ___   120 ___!

130 ___   14 ___ 10 ___ 7 ___   10 ___ 600 ___ 600 ___.

MY NEW MATH WORDS: About Subtraction

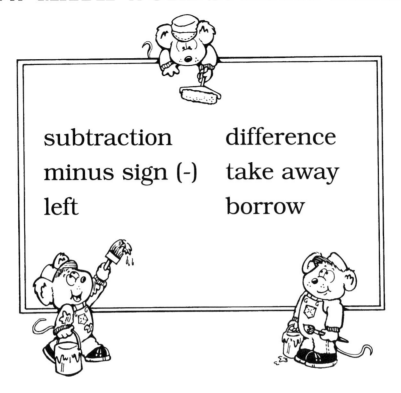

subtraction   difference

minus sign (-)   take away

left   borrow

Draw lines connecting the old math words below to the pictures, numbers, or symbols they describe.

add   =

                                           +

3-digit number

                                           5 3 7

tens   10 + 5 + 3

plus sign

equal sign

Skills: math literacy, vocabulary building, visual discrimination

When you take numbers away from each other, it is called **subtraction**. The picture symbol used for subtraction is called a **minus sign (–)**. Look at the pictures below to do some subtraction problems.

Nine ducks were swimming in a pond.

Six ducks swam away.

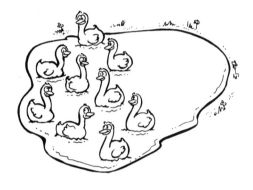

How many ducks were swimming in the pond? _____

How many ducks swam away? _____

How many ducks are left? **Subtract** them. _____

When you subtract one number from another, you get the **difference**. Here is your **subtraction problem**:

$$9 \text{ s} - 6 \text{ s} = 3 \text{ s}$$

Skills: 1-digit subtraction, math symbols, writing equations, word problems

1-Digit Subtraction

Jessica takes care of animals in a pet store. Sometimes she takes groups of animals outside for some fresh air. Look at each picture below and figure out how many she leaves in the pet store. Subtract the number of animals she takes outside from the total number of animals. This number is called the **difference**. Write the **difference** on the line provided.

$-$ _____ = _____ **left**.

$-$ _____ = _____ **left**.

$-$ _____ = _____ **left**.

TOGETHER TIME: Ask an adult to take you on a trip to the pet store. When you go, bring a pencil and a piece of paper with you. At the pet store, count all the dogs you see. Write that number on your paper. Then count all the cats you see and write down that number. Did you see more dogs or more cats? How many more of one animal than the other animal did you see? Have your adult friend help you set up a subtraction problem to find out your answer.

Skills: 1-digit subtraction, word problems

Let's practice subtracting 2-digit numbers. Look at the rules below.

> ## How to subtract 2-digit numbers:
> 1. Subtract the numbers in the ones' place.
> 2. If you are subtracting a larger number from a smaller number, borrow 1 ten for 10 ones.
> 3. Subtract the numbers in the tens' place.
> 4. Write the difference.

First subtract the ones' place.

$$\begin{array}{r} 2\ 5 \\ -\ \ 7 \\ \hline \end{array}$$

7 is larger than 5. We borrow from the tens' place when we are subtracting a larger number from a smaller number.

We can borrow 1 ten from the tens' place.

$$\begin{array}{r} 1\!\!\!\!/2 \quad 15+10=15 \\ -\ \ 7 \quad\quad 8 \\ \hline 8 \end{array}$$

Think: 2 -1=1) We can add 10 ones to the ones' place to get 15 ones. 15 minus 7 equals 8.

Then subtract the tens' place.

$$\begin{array}{r} 1\!\!\!\!/2 \quad 15 \\ -\ 0\ \ 7 \\ \hline 1\ 8 \end{array}$$

Subtract 0 tens from 1 ten to get 1.

The answer is the **difference**.

Here's a subtraction game called "Less Than." Look at the pictures on the left side of the page. Count the number of items in each picture and write that number below its picture. Then subtract the number on the right side of the page from the number you wrote. The first one is done for you.

5

2 less = ___3___

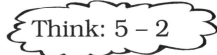

Think: 5 – 2

_____

5 less = _____

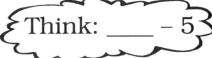

Think: ___ – 5

_____

6 less = _____

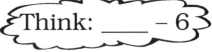

Think: ___ – 6

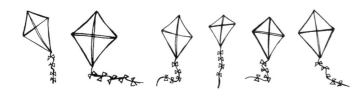

_____

4 less = _____

Think: ___ – ___

Skills: 1- and 2-digit subtraction, writing subtraction equations

GRADE BOOSTER!

There are 9 different kinds of toy vehicles in the toy box. Use your favorite color crayon to color each truck in the box.

How many trucks did you color? _____
How many vehicles are not colored? _____
Write a subtraction equation to help you find out.

_____ *less than* _____ = _____

Think: How many vehicles in all? _____
How many did I color? _____

Here is a subtraction game for you to play. You have 30¢ to buy some toys.

When you buy a toy, put an **X** over it, then write its price in the table below. The first toy is crossed out for you. It costs 14¢, so you now have 16¢ left. Each time you buy a toy, subtract it until you have *no more money* to spend.

30¢	-	14¢	=	16¢
16¢	-	____¢	=	____¢
____¢	-	____¢	=	____¢
____¢	-	____¢	=	____¢
____¢	-	____¢	=	____¢
____¢	-	____¢	=	____¢

Skills: 1- and 2-digit subtraction, money facts, problem solving

Read each subtraction story. Then solve the problems.
Write the differences on the lines provided.

Marilyn bought 15 apples to make apple pies. She put
12 apples in the refrigerator.

How many apples were left on the counter? _____

Think: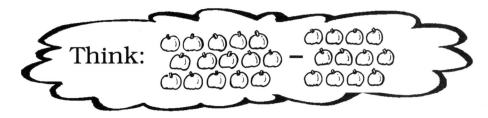

20 pumpkins are sitting
on the fence. 6 fall off.
How many are left? _____

Think:

23 doves were flying to the park.
12 turned around and flew
in the other direction.
How many were left?

_____

Think:

GRADE BOOSTER!

*Write your own subtraction story like the ones
above about your favorite animal or animals.
Give the problem to a friend to solve.*

It's time to learn 3-digit subtraction. Look at the rules below.

How to subtract **3-digit numbers:**
1. **Subract the numbers in the ones' place.**
2. **If you are subtracting a larger number from a smaller number, borrow 1 ten for 10 ones.**
3. **Subtract the numbers in the tens' place.**
4. **If you are subtracting a larger number from a smaller number, borrow 1 hundred for 10 tens.**
5. **Subtract the numbers in the hundreds' place.**
6. **Write the difference.**

First subtract the ones' place.

$$3\,4\overset{4}{5}\,\overset{1}{5}\,7\ \ +10=17$$
$$-\,1\,5\,8 \underline{}\ 9$$
$$9$$

8 is larger than 7. Borrow 1 ten for 10 ones. Now you have 4 tens left and 17 ones. Subtract 8 from 17. This equals 9.

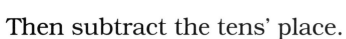

Then subtract the tens' place.

$$2\,\overset{14}{3}\overset{4}{5}\,7\ \ 14-5=9$$
$$-\,1\ \ 5\,8$$
$$9\,9$$

5 is larger than 4. Borrow 1 hundred for 10 tens. Now you have 2 hundreds left and 14 tens. Subtract 5 tens from 14 tens. This equals 9.

Next subtract the hundreds' place.

$$1\ \overset{2}{3}\,5\,7$$
$$-\,1\,5\,8$$
$$1\,9\,9$$

Subtract 1 hundred from 2 hundreds. This equals 1. The answer is the difference.

Skills: 3-digit subtraction problems, borrowing tens and hundreds

Now let's practice subtracting 3-digit numbers. Follow the steps on page 220 to complete each problem. If you need more room, copy the problems onto another piece of paper and then solve them. The first one has been done for you.

```
  9 2 7
- 5 9 8
  3 2 9
```

```
  2 8 1
- 1 9 3
```

```
  4 8 6
- 2 8 7
```

```
  6 2 1
- 3 8 3
```

```
  9 6 3
- 1 7 4
```

```
  6 1 0
- 5 9 9
```

GRADE BOOSTER!

How many days are there in a year? _____ What if the year is a leap year. Then how many days are there? _____ Do you know what a leap year is? If not, ask a parent or other adult friend. How many days are there in 2 regular years?

_____

How many days are there in 1 regular year and 1 leap year? _____

3-Digit Subtraction

Complete the subtraction problems to match each character to his or her proper hat. When you are done, draw a line from each character to his or her hat.

$$632 - 306$$

$$346 - 184$$

$$416 - 223$$

$$444 - 175$$

$$577 - 326$$

$$537 - 130$$

$$312 - 145$$

$$227 - 122$$

193   251   326   269

105   162   167   407

TOGETHER TIME: Ask an adult to make up some more 3-digit subtraction problems for you to complete. When you're done, have the adult check them.

Skills: 3-digit subtraction

LET'S REVIEW: SUBTRACTION

Write the difference.

Answer: _____

38 pennies are in the bag.

18 pennies are taken out.

How many pennies are left? _____

How many are 2 less? _____

What is the difference between the two scores?_____

Do you have to borrow? ____ yes ____ no

Award Certificate
I am a Wizard
in
Subtraction

_____

(my name)

How many more ●s than ⊘s are there?

_____ – _____ = _____

MY NEW MATH WORDS:
About Multiplication

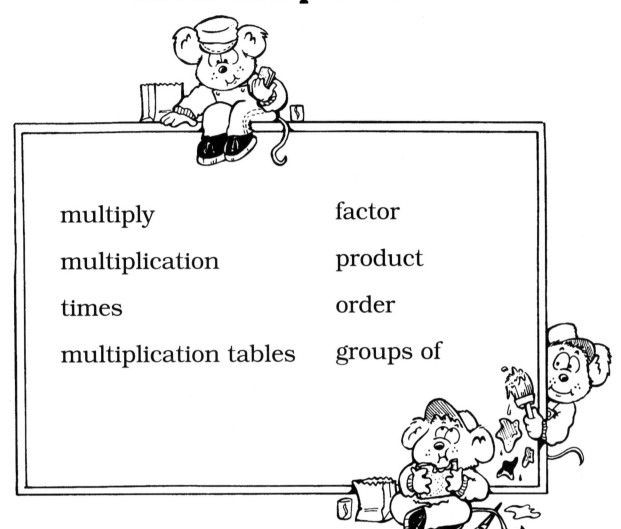

multiply   factor

multiplication   product

times   order

multiplication tables   groups of

GRADE BOOSTER!

2

Draw a line from each old math word to the number or symbol it describes.

minus sign   2-digit number   3-digit number   difference

324   –   81 – 57   22

Multiplication

When we **multiply,** we are actually adding two or more numbers together. In fact, **multiplication** is really a short way of adding. The numbers we multiply are called **factors**. The picture symbol for multiplication is a **times sign (x)**. Look at this example:

Here are 3 bags of pears. Each bag has 2 pears inside it. How many pears are there altogether? To solve this problem, you can add all 3 bags of pears together.

 = <u>6 pears</u>

OR

Solve it using **multiplication**.
First identify the **factors**. There are two **factors**: **3** (for 3 bags) and **2** (for 2 pears inside each bag).

We write the **multiplication problem** like this: 3 x 2. When we multiply the **factors,** 3 x 2, we get the **product**. The **product** is the answer: 6.

We write the multiplication in an **equation**:

$$3 \quad x \quad 2 \quad = \quad 6$$

We say the **equation** like this: "three times two equals six."

The order of the factors does not change the product. For example, we can also write:

$$2 \quad x \quad 3 \quad = \quad 6$$

We say the **equation** like this: "two times three equals six."

Skills: 1-digit multiplication, math symbols, writing multiplication equations

You can learn all the **factors** and their **products** for the numbers 1 to 10 by memorizing **multiplication tables**. A **multiplication table** looks like this:

On the left side are the two **factors** to **multiply**.

The Ones' Table

$1 \times 0 = 0$
$1 \times 1 = 1$

On the right side is the **product**.

Here are the **multiplication tables** for the numbers 1 through 5. Say the **factors** and **products** out loud: "One times zero is zero, one times one is one," and so on.

The Ones' Table

$1 \times 0 = 0$
$1 \times 1 = 1$
$1 \times 2 = 2$
$1 \times 3 = 3$
$1 \times 4 = 4$
$1 \times 5 = 5$
$1 \times 6 = 6$
$1 \times 7 = 7$
$1 \times 8 = 8$
$1 \times 9 = 9$
$1 \times 10 = 10$

The Twos' Table

$2 \times 0 = 0$
$2 \times 1 = 2$
$2 \times 2 = 4$
$2 \times 3 = 6$
$2 \times 4 = 8$
$2 \times 5 = 10$
$2 \times 6 = 12$
$2 \times 7 = 14$
$2 \times 8 = 16$
$2 \times 9 = 18$
$2 \times 10 = 20$

The Threes' Table

$3 \times 0 = 0$
$3 \times 1 = 3$
$3 \times 2 = 6$
$3 \times 3 = 9$
$3 \times 4 = 12$
$3 \times 5 = 15$
$3 \times 6 = 18$
$3 \times 7 = 21$
$3 \times 8 = 24$
$3 \times 9 = 27$
$3 \times 10 = 30$

The Fours' Table

$4 \times 0 = 0$
$4 \times 1 = 4$
$4 \times 2 = 8$
$4 \times 3 = 12$
$4 \times 4 = 16$
$4 \times 5 = 20$
$4 \times 6 = 24$
$4 \times 7 = 28$
$4 \times 8 = 32$
$4 \times 9 = 36$
$4 \times 10 = 40$

The Fives' Table

$5 \times 0 = 0$
$5 \times 1 = 5$
$5 \times 2 = 10$
$5 \times 3 = 15$
$5 \times 4 = 20$
$5 \times 5 = 25$
$5 \times 6 = 30$
$5 \times 7 = 35$
$5 \times 8 = 40$
$5 \times 9 = 45$
$5 \times 10 = 50$

FIVE TIMES FIVE IS TWENTY-FIVE.

Skills: using the multiplication tables: 1–5

The Sixes' Table	The Sevens' Table	The Eights' Table
6 x 0 = 0	7 x 0 = 0	8 x 0 = 0
6 x 1 = 6	7 x 1 = 7	8 x 1 = 8
6 x 2 = 12	7 x 2 = 14	8 x 2 = 16
6 x 3 = 18	7 x 3 = 21	8 x 3 = 24
6 x 4 = 24	7 x 4 = 28	8 x 4 = 32
6 x 5 = 30	7 x 5 = 35	8 x 5 = 40
6 x 6 = 36	7 x 6 = 42	8 x 6 = 48
6 x 7 = 42	7 x 7 = 49	8 x 7 = 56
6 x 8 = 48	7 x 8 = 56	8 x 8 = 64
6 x 9 = 54	7 x 9 = 63	8 x 9 = 72
6 x 10 = 60	7 x 10 = 70	8 x 10 = 80

The Nines' Table	The Tens' Table
9 x 0 = 0	10 x 0 = 0
9 x 1 = 9	10 x 1 = 10
9 x 2 = 18	10 x 2 = 20
9 x 3 = 27	10 x 3 = 30
9 x 4 = 36	10 x 4 = 40
9 x 5 = 45	10 x 5 = 50
9 x 6 = 54	10 x 6 = 60
9 x 7 = 63	10 x 7 = 70
9 x 8 = 72	10 x 8 = 80
9 x 9 = 81	10 x 9 = 90
9 x 10 = 90	10 x 10 = 100

TOGETHER TIME: Find some scissors and construction paper. Ask an adult to help you cut out 100 2" x 2" squares. Then, with your adult friend, make flashcards of all the multiplication tables. On one side write the factors, and on the other side write the product. Practice learning your multiplication tables by looking at the factors, then saying the correct product.

Here are two special rules to keep in mind:

(1.) When you multiply a number by 0, the product is **always** 0.

1 x 0 = 0   **2 x 0 = 0**   **3 x 0 = _____**

(2.) When you multiply a number by 1, the product is **always** that number.

1 x 1 = 1   **1 x 2 = 2**   **1 x 3 = _____**

Now use these rules to help you solve this problem.
How many sails are there on these 3 boats?
3 boats times 1 sail on each boat equals _____,
or 3 x 1 = _____

GRADE BOOSTER!

2

How many of these problems can you complete in 30 seconds? Ask an adult to time you for 30 seconds while you solve the multiplication problems.

6	3	2	1	5	4	7
x 0	x 1	x 0	x 1	x 0	x 0	x 1

6	3	2	1	5	4	7
x 1	x 0	x 1	x 0	x 1	x 1	x 0

Skills: multiplying by 0s and 1s

Use the multiplication tables on pages 227 and 228 to help you solve these multiplication problems.

1 x 1 =

1 x 3 =

2 x 0 =

2 x 4 =

2 x 6 =

3 x 2 =

3 x 5 =

4 x 3 =

4 x 4 =

5 x 2 =

5 x 5 =

5 x 6 =

6 x 1 =

6 x 3 =

6 x 5 =

7 x 3 =

7 x 4 =

7 x 6 =

8 x 3 =

8 x 6 =

8 x 8 =

9 x 2 =

9 x 4 =

9 x 6 =

10 x 0 =

10 x 2 =

10 x 4 =

Skills: using multiplication tables: 1–10

Are you ready to do some more multiplication? Look at the pictures below. Write the **factors,** the **equation,** and the **product.** Then solve the problem. Use the tables on pages 227 and 228 if you need help.

Here are 4 fish bowls.
Each bowl has 2 fish.
There are 4 groups of 2 fish.
How many fish are there altogether?

Write the **factors** here: _____ _____

Write the **equation** here: _____ **x** _____ **=** _____

Write the **product** here: _____ fish altogether.

Here are 5 plates of cookies.
Each plate has 2 cookies.
There are 5 groups of 2 cookies.
How many cookies are there altogether?

Write the **factors** here: _____ _____

Write the **equation** here:

_____ **x** _____ **=** _____

Write the **product** here: _____ cookies altogether.

Colleen practices her multiplication with playing cards. Look at the number on each card. Then multiply it by how many cards there are. The first one is done for you.

<u> 9 </u> x <u> 3 </u> = <u>27</u>

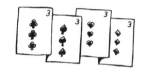

<u> 3 </u> x <u> 4 </u> = ___

___ x ___ = ___

___ x ___ = ___

___ x ___ = ___

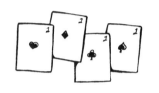

___ x ___ = ___

GRADE BOOSTER!

*Now it's time to create your own playing cards to multiply. Write numbers on the blank cards below. For each set of cards, make sure to write the same number on every card. Then multiply your cards: the number of cards times the numbers on the cards. Write the **factors** and **products** in the space provided.*

___ x ___ = ___

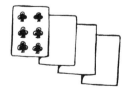

___ x ___ = ___

Skills: identifying factors, writing multiplication problems, finding products

Here are some multiplication story problems. Read each one and then write the **factors** and **products** on the lines provided.

Andrea got 10 points on 3 math tests. How many points did she earn altogether?

____ points **x** ____ tests **=** ____ points altogether

There are 4 bunnies in the garden. Each bunny ate 2 carrots. How many carrots did they eat altogether?

____ bunnies **x** ____ carrots **=** ____ carrots altogether

There are 5 bears on the ice hockey team. Each team member has 2 skates. How many skates does the whole team have altogether?

____ bears **x** ____ skates **=** ____ skates altogether

LET'S REVIEW: MULTIPLICATION

How many bananas are there altogether? Write the factors and product.

Jose has 9 baskets. Each basket has 6 apples. How many apples are there altogether?

4 x _____ = _____

_____ apples in all

Multiply by 4s.

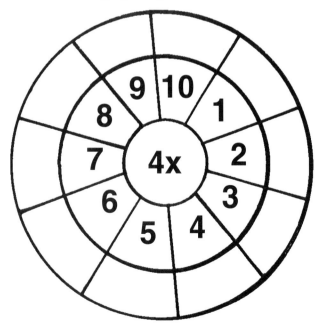

Solve these problems.

6	7	8	9	10
x 1	x 0	x 1	x 0	x 1

Skills: identifying factors, writing multiplication problems, finding products

Award Certificate
I am Great
at
Multiplication

_____

(my name)

How many leaves are in the jungle?

____ trees **x** ____ leaves = ____ leaves altogether

MY NEW MATH WORDS:
About Fractions

fraction	one-half, ½
part	one-third, ⅓
whole	one-fourth, ¼
equal	one-fifth, ⅕
	one-sixth, ⅙

Draw a line to connect each old math word on the left to its **definition** (what the word means) on the right.

product	numbers you multiply together
multiplication	answer in multiplication
factors	a short way of adding
group	multiplication symbol
x	more than one of anything

Skills: math literacy, vocabulary building, visual discrimination

Billy bakes cakes. He cuts his cakes into **equal parts**. Each **equal part** is called a **fraction**. Let's see how many parts he cut up.

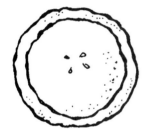

one whole
1
1 whole

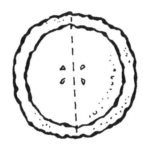

one-half
½
2 equal parts

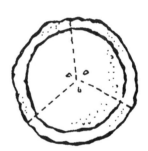

one-third
⅓
3 equal parts

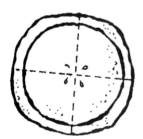

one-fourth
¼
4 equal parts

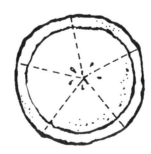

one-fifth
⅕
5 equal parts

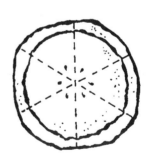

one-sixth
⅙
6 equal parts

Skills: identifying fractions: ½, ⅓, ¼, ⅕, and ⅙ in words and numbers

Fractions

Today Billy is cutting his cakes into halves (½) and thirds (⅓). Look at each cake. One piece is shaded. Figure out what fraction of the whole cake is shaded. The first one is done for you.

What fraction is the shaded piece? __½__

What fraction is the shaded piece?_____

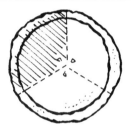

What fraction is the shaded piece?_____

What fraction is the shaded piece?_____

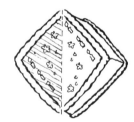

What fraction is the shaded piece?_____

GRADE BOOSTER!

Use your pencil to shade the part or parts of the circles below so they look like fractions. Then write the fractions on the lines.

 = _____

 = _____

Skills: identifying halves and thirds in words and numbers

Here is the fraction one-fourth (¼).
1 of the 4 parts is shaded.

Here is the fraction one-fifth (⅕).
1 of the 5 parts is shaded.

Here is the fraction one-sixth (⅙)
1 of the 6 parts is shaded.

Check (✓) off all the correct pictures for these fractions.

One-fourth (¼)

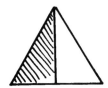 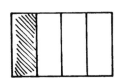  

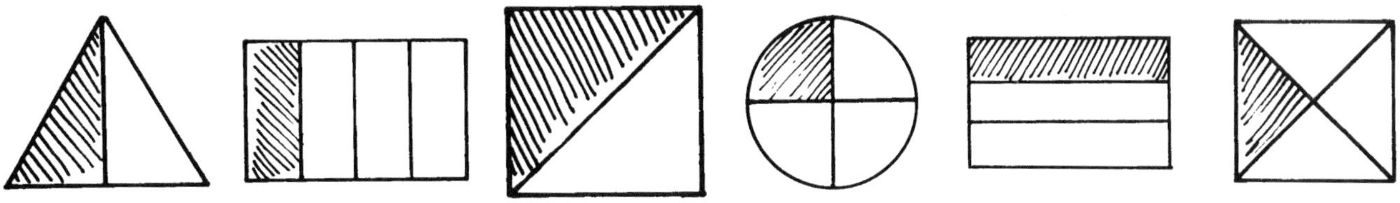

One-fifth (⅕)

  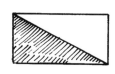  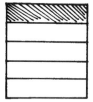

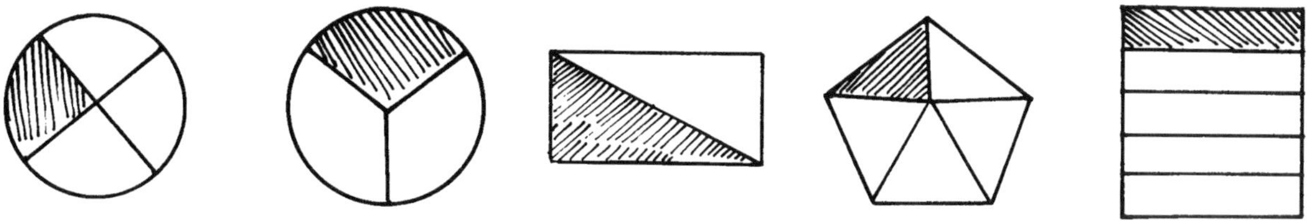

One-sixth (⅙)

   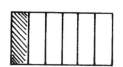 

Fractions

Now it's your turn to draw the parts that make up each fraction.

$\dfrac{2}{6}$ of the dogs have spots. Draw the spots on the correct number of dogs.

$\dfrac{3}{5}$ of the kittens have whiskers. Draw the whiskers on the correct number of kittens.

$\dfrac{4}{5}$ of the bunnies have tails. Draw the tails on the correct number of bunnies.

$\dfrac{3}{4}$ of the camels have humps. Draw the humps on the correct number of camels.

Skills: identifying fractions for fourths, fifths, and sixths

LET'S REVIEW: FRACTIONS

Write the letter answer, A, B, C, or D, on the lines below.

A. $\dfrac{1}{5}$ B. $\dfrac{2}{4}$ C. $\dfrac{2}{3}$ D. $\dfrac{1}{2}$

What fraction is shaded?

Answer:_____

What fraction of the dogs have spots?

Answer:_____

What fraction of the milk in the glass did Betsy drink?

Answer: _____

A large pizza was cut into 4 pieces. Joan ate 1 piece. Billy ate 1 piece. How many pieces are left?

Answer:_____

Skills: identifying fractions

Award Certificate

GOOD WORK!

WOW! HURRAY!

1ST

_____

(my name)

Is a Fraction Pro!

Draw a line matching the fraction on the left with its picture on the right!

1/2

5/6

1/3

2/4

4/8

Certificate of Completion

and Special Secret Message
for:

_____
(my name)

1	2	3	4	5	6	7	8	9	10	11	12
H	C	E	F	I	M	N	R	S	T	U	A

Each boxed number has a letter that goes with it. Put these letters in the blanks below to show the secret message. The first blank is filled in for you!

$\dfrac{I}{5}$ $\dfrac{}{12}$ $\dfrac{}{6}$ $\dfrac{}{10}$ $\dfrac{}{3}$ $\dfrac{}{8}$ $\dfrac{}{8}$ $\dfrac{}{5}$ $\dfrac{}{4}$ $\dfrac{}{5}$ $\dfrac{}{2}$

$\dfrac{}{12}$ $\dfrac{}{10}$ $\dfrac{}{6}$ $\dfrac{}{12}$ $\dfrac{}{10}$ $\dfrac{}{1}$!

Math
Puzzles & Games

This section offers a variety of games and activities that make learning math fun. It reviews counting and estimating, addition, subtraction, multiplication, and division through fractions, with entertaining exercises in interpreting clues, organizing data, and reaching conclusions through reasoning.

This section is full of fun puzzles and games to help me practice my math skills!

LEAPFROG

When you count by twos, you skip every other number. Look at the frogs below. Then, starting with the frog marked 2, play leapfrog by circling every other frog. When you are finished, read the circled numbers in order out loud. Then, using crayons, color the circled frogs brown. Color the rest of the frogs green.

TOGETHER TIME: Get a handful of pennies from your piggy bank or from an adult friend, then find a clock or a watch. Have your adult friend time you counting the pennies one by one on a table. Then have your adult friend time you counting the pennies by twos. Which was faster? Time your adult friend counting the pennies both ways.

Skills: number recognition, counting by twos, verbalizing numbers

FLYING FIVES

Billy collects models of airplanes, space shuttles, rockets, and anything else that can fly. Help Billy count how many flying toys he has by counting them by fives. Begin by counting out 5 toys and then circling that group of 5 toys. Continue until all the toys are contained in a circle of 5. Then count the circled groups out loud by fives.

GRADE BOOSTER!

Look at the toys above. Some of them are models of flying machines that are designed to go into space. How many can go into space? Using a blue crayon, color the toys that can go into space.

RIDDLING CHEETAH

The riddling cheetah loves to tell riddles. Follow the directions below to find the answer to his riddle. Using crayons, fill in the correct squares with any color you like.

Which number tells you how many letters are in its name?

In row 1, color the B and D squares.

In row 2, color the B and D squares.

In row 3, color the B, C, D, and E squares.

In row 4, color the D square.

In row 5, color the D square.

	A	B	C	D	E	F
Row 1						
Row 2						
Row 3						
Row 4						
Row 5						

Skills: grid maneuvering, number recognition

WHAT COMES NEXT?

Look closely at each row of numbers below. Then decide what number should come next. Write that number in the watermelon at the end of the row. Make sure that the number follows the pattern of that row.

2	4	6	8	
5	10	15	20	
12	14	16	18	
65	70	75	80	
101	103	105	107	

GRADE BOOSTER!

Patterns of numbers are all around us. They're even in sports! In football, a touchdown counts for 7 points. If a team scored 3 touchdowns in a game, how many points would the team have after each touchdown? _____

DIGITS

Read the questions below and write the answers on the lines provided. Then draw a line from each answer to the kind of number it is on the right. For help, read the box at the bottom of the page.

How old are you? _____

How many people are in your family? _____

How many days are in each year? _____

How many toes do you have? _____

How many legs does a spider have? _____

How many teeth do you have? _____

How many forks are in your kitchen? _____

1-digit number

2-digit number

3-digit number

HELP BOX: A digit is a whole number. The numbers 0, 1, 2, 3, 4, 5, 6, 7, 8, and 9 are **1-digit numbers**. They are made up of only one number. Numbers between 10 and 99 are **2-digit numbers**. The numbers 10, 26, 45, and 78 are examples of 2-digit numbers. They are made up of two numbers. Numbers between 100 and 999 are **3-digit numbers**. The numbers 112, 543, and 773 are examples of 3-digit numbers. They are made up of three numbers.

Skills: identifying 1-, 2-, and 3-digit numbers

FLAG FUN

Look at the box with numbers below.
Then follow the directions to create a flag.

Color the section with 1-digit numbers red.

Color the section with 2-digit numbers blue.

Color the section with 3-digit numbers yellow.

111	379	980	203
10	12	99	50
3	8	1	7

GRADE BOOSTER!

Use an atlas or an encyclopedia to answer these questions: What country does this flag represent? What continent is it on? What is the capital of that country?

TENS PLACE TANGO

Look at the number 10. It has two digits: 1 and 0. This means it has two **place values:** a 1 in the tens' place and a 0 in the ones' place. Using crayons, follow the directions to create a flag in the boxes below.

Color all the sections with a 7 in the tens' place blue.

Color all the sections with a 3 in the tens' place white.

Color all the sections with a 9 in the tens' place red.

71	37	96
73	39	95

GRADE BOOSTER!

Use an atlas or an encyclopedia to answer these questions: What country does this flag represent? What continent is it on? What is the capital of that country? What other countries have the same colors in their flag?

Skills: identifying place values for tens

SATURDAY IN THE PARK

Look at the park scene below. In each pair of boxes, write the number of similar items you see near those boxes. Then, using crayons, color the numbers in the ones' place yellow. Color the numbers in the tens' place orange.

ZOO PLACES

Look at the picture below. Write the number of animals in each cage in the sign below the animals' cage. Then, using crayons, color the number in the ones' place green. Color the number in the tens' place yellow.

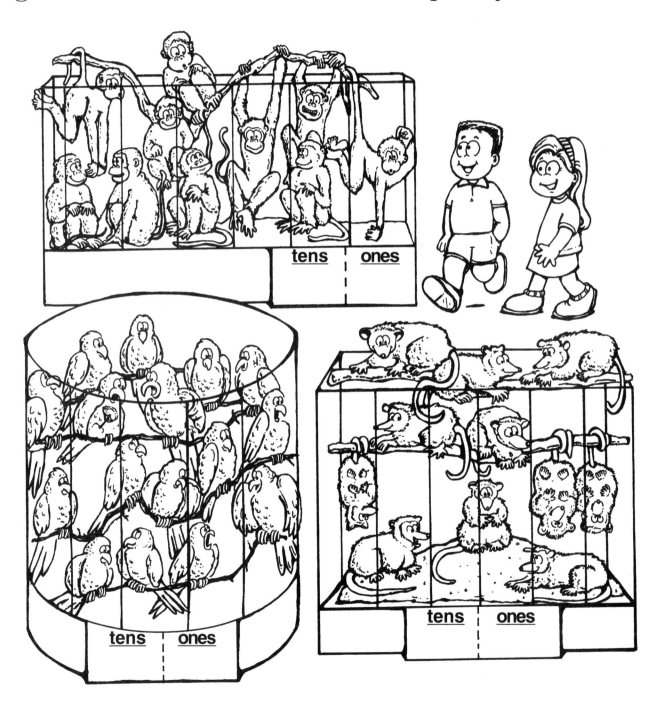

Skills: identifying place values for ones and tens

MORE FLAG FUN

3-digit numbers have three place values. They have a number in the ones' place, tens' place, and **hundreds' place**. Use what you know about place values to color in the flag. Follow the directions below.

Color the sections that have numbers with a 7 in the hundreds' place green.

Color the sections that have numbers with a 5 in the tens' place yellow.

Color the sections that have numbers with a 3 in the ones' place black.

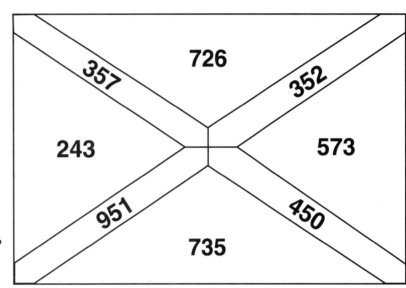

357 726 352
243   573
951 735 450

GRADE BOOSTER!

Use an atlas or an encyclopedia to answer these questions: What country does this flag represent? What is that country's capital city?

Skills: identifying place values for hundreds, tens, and ones

ESTIMATE OR COUNT?

Sometimes there are so many items in a group that it would take a *really* long time to count them all. How can you find out how many items there are when there are so many? You can **estimate,** or guess. If you need to, you can go back and **count** each item to get the actual number.

Look at the picture below. How many leaves do you think are on the tree? Write your estimate on the line provided. Now count the number of leaves. Was your estimate more, less, or exactly the same as the actual number?

My estimate: _____

Actual number of leaves: _____

BEST ESTIMATE

Sometimes there are so many items in a group, it would be almost impossible to count them all. To figure out how many items there are, you must **estimate,** or guess.

Look at the amounts below. Use a green crayon to circle the amounts that you would estimate instead of count. Use a purple crayon to put a square around the amounts that you would count.

Number of stars
in the sky

Number of kids in
your math class

Number of grains of
sand on the beach

Number of days
in a week

Number of cars in
your toy box

Number of planets
in our solar system

Number of bubbles
in your soda

Number of buttons
on your telephone

TOGETHER TIME: With an adult friend, visit a library and find out how **astronomers,** or scientists who study stars and planets and other things in space, figure out how many stars are in the sky. Do astronomers estimate or count?

LET'S REVIEW

Jacob thinks he understands digits, place values, and estimation, but he wants to be sure. Jacob asks his dad to ask him some questions. Can you help Jacob by writing in the answer he should give his dad?

Skills: identifying 2- and 3-digit numbers, place values, estimation

CONGRATULATIONS!

_____

(my name)

Knows Numbers and
Is Ready for

ADDING IN THE OCEAN

Look at the picture below. The ocean is empty! Fill in the scene by drawing 5 fish, 2 crabs, and 1 octopus. Then answer the questions on the next page.

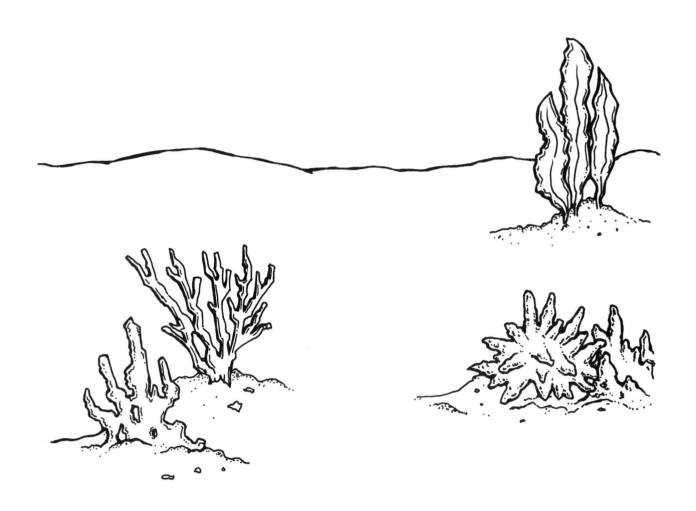

TOGETHER TIME: Show the addition problem below to an adult friend. Tell your friend that you know how to magically make the numbers add up to 10!
Hint: To make the numbers add up to 10, just turn the whole problem upside down!

$$1 + 6$$

Skills: 1-digit addition, math symbols, writing equations, word problems

How many fish and crabs are there in all?

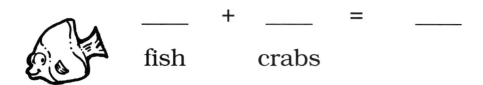

___ + ___ = ___

fish   crabs

How many crabs and octopuses are there in all?

___ + ___ = ___

crabs   octopuses

How many fish and octopuses are there in all?

___ + ___ = ___

fish   octopuses

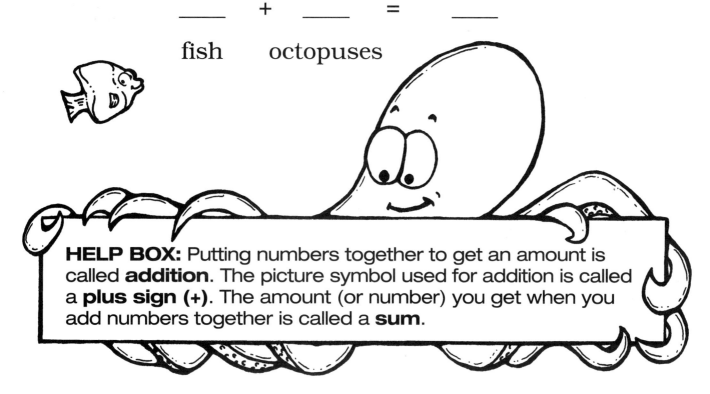

HELP BOX: Putting numbers together to get an amount is called **addition**. The picture symbol used for addition is called a **plus sign (+)**. The amount (or number) you get when you add numbers together is called a **sum**.

Skills: 1-digit addition, math symbols, writing equations, word problems

WORD MATH

Look at the words in **bold** below. Count the letters in each word, then write the number of letters in each word on the blank lines. Next, add the number of letters in each pair of words and write the total on the line next to **sum**.

How many letters are in **cherry**? ____

How many letters are in **tree**? ____

             sum: ____

Now write a word that has that many

letters in it: _____

How many letters are in **flower**? ____

How many letters are in **acrobat**? ____

             sum: ____

Now write a word that has that many

letters in it: _____

Hint: Look through some books that have long words until you find a word with the right number of letters.

GRADE BOOSTER!

2

If the cost, in dollars, of a pizza and a hamburger were equal to the number of letters in each word, how much would both cost altogether? ____ If you had $4 and a friend gave you $8, would you have enough to buy both? If yes, how much money would you have left over, if any? ____ If no, how much more money would you need? ____

Skills: 1-digit addition, research, creativity

RECYCLING NUMBERS

Zack and Isabel believe in using things, such as plastic bags and glass jars, again and again. This is called **recycling**. Zack and Isabel also recycle numbers! Below are four pairs of numbers. In each pair, a number from the first number has been **recycled,** or used again, in the second number. Find the recycled number and write it in the space next to the pair.

670 and **405** ___ **961** and **576** ___

376 and **345** ___ **218** and **843** ___

Now add the four recycled numbers. What is the sum? Write the answer in the dinosaur bone.

___ + ___ + ___ + ___ =

LADYBUG ADDITION

Look at the big sunflower below. Notice that each leaf has a different number of ladybugs on it. Draw a line to connect two leaves that have a total of 7 ladybugs on them. There are three pairs of leaves that combine to make 7 ladybugs. Can you find and connect all three pairs?

TOGETHER TIME: Get a deck of cards. With an adult friend, take all the kings, queens, and jacks out of the deck. Deal 20 cards to your adult friend and 20 cards to yourself. Take turns picking two cards at a time out of your 20. Add the numbers on the two cards and write down the sum. Do this until you have used up all your cards. Add up all the sums each of you got. The person with the higher total is the winner.

Skills: 1- and 2-digit addition

ROAD TRIP

Look at the map below. If you wanted to drive from Calabasas to Timbuktu in a hurry, which route would be the fastest? How many miles is it? To find the answer, add the numbers along each route. The smallest number is the fastest route! If you need help adding, read the help box below.

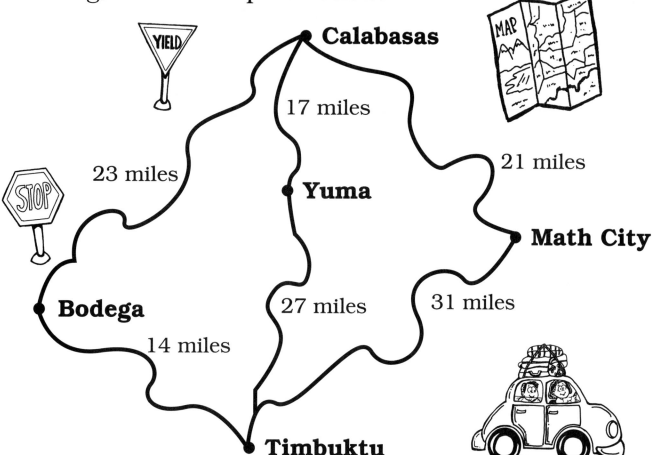

HELP BOX: How to add **2-digit numbers:**
1. Add the numbers in the ones' column.
2. If there are more than 10 ones, you need to **carry**. Write the ones in the ones' column, then carry over the tens to the tens' column.
3. Add the numbers in the tens' column.
4. Write the sum, or total.

$$\begin{array}{r} {}^{1}16 \\ +\ 25 \\ \hline 41 \end{array}$$

LINE UP THE POOL CUE

Philadelphia Fats is a great pool player. If Fats had numbers on his pool table like the ones on the table below, he could lay his cue stick across the table and add up the three numbers the cue touched. The dotted lines show Fats all the ways he could do this. Which way would he have to lay his cue stick on the table to get the highest number? Draw a solid line to show Fats where to lay his cue stick.

Skills: 1- and 2-digit addition, carrying tens

CRACK THE CODE

Landon Lizard loves to crack codes. Help him crack the code below by solving each of the addition problems above the blank boxes. Then check the code breaker to find out what letter goes in the box below each sum. The letters in the boxes will answer the riddle below.

CODE BREAKER				
42	**11**	**41**	**70**	**93**
E	U	B	L	M

Riddle: What kind of bee is hard to understand?

77	7	81	33	53	15
+16	+4	+12	+8	+17	+27

A ▯ ▯ ▯ ▯ ▯ ▯ BEE

ANNIVERSARY PRESENT

Rachel and Zoe want to buy their parents an anniversary present. Read the following information and decide what they can buy if they put their money together. **Hint:** Use addition to find out. If you need help, see the help box below.

Rachel has $153. Zoe has $251.

How much money do they have? _____

Which present can they buy their parents? _____

HELP BOX: How to add **3-digit numbers:**
1. Add the numbers in the ones' place.
2. If there are more than 10 ones, carry to the tens' place.
3. Add the numbers in the tens' place.
4. If there are more than 10 tens, carry to the hundreds' place.
5. Write the sum, or total.

Skills: 3-digit addition, carrying tens, problem solving, deduction, money facts

EVAN'S DRUM SET

Evan wants to buy a new drum set that costs $550. To help him buy his drum set, Evan's family all gave him some money. Evan kept a record of how much money each family member gave him. Look at Evan's record below. Help him add up the money to see if he now has enough money to buy the drum set.

Mom and Dad	**$200**
Michele	**$1**
Aunt Suzy	**$50**
Grandma	**$100**
Uncle Russ	**$150**
Aunt Laurie	**$50**
Total	**$ _____**

Evan's record (handwritten note):

mom and dad $200
michele $1
Aunt Suzy $50
Grandma $100
Uncle Russ $150
Aunt Laurie $50
total $ _____

Does Evan have enough money for his new drum set? Circle the answer.

YES   NO

If the answer is yes, how much money does Evan have left over? _____

If the answer is no, how much more money does Evan need? _____

LET'S REVIEW: ADDITION

Look at the crossword puzzle below. Instead of filling in the boxes with letters to make words, you are going to fill in the boxes with numbers! Read each numbered clue to find out what to write in the boxes.

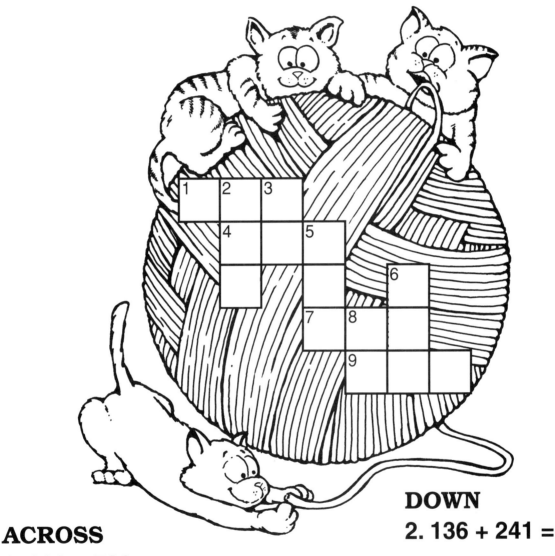

DOWN

2. 136 + 241 =

3. 8 + 2 =

5. 409 + 3 =

6. 756 + 211 =

8. 29 + 6 =

ACROSS

1. 210 + 521 =

4. 398 + 306 =

7. 216 + 20 =

9. 391 + 183 =

Skills: 1-, 2-, and 3-digit addition with carrying

CHARLIE'S SEASIDE DRIVE

One day Charlie took a drive along the seashore. He took many pictures of the things he saw. Then he put the pictures in the order that he took them for you to see, too. Use the pictures on the next page to answer the questions below.

Start at the picture of the whale.

Go forward 2 pictures and back 1.

What do you see? _____

Now go forward 5 pictures and back 2.

What do you see? _____

Now go back 1 picture and forward 3.

What do you see? _____

Skills: 1-digit addition, 1-digit subtraction, problem solving

TOGETHER TIME: With an adult friend, find some photographs that were taken during your last outing or vacation. Line them up like Charlie did to play this game with your own pictures.

Skills: 1-digit addition, 1-digit subtraction, problem solving

CODE BREAKER

Chris and Carla are talking about school. To find out Carla's answer to Chris's question, solve the subtraction problems below. Then match your answers to the correct letter using the secret code box. If you need help with subtraction, look at the help box below.

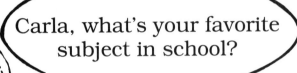

Carla, what's your favorite subject in school?

SECRET CODE BOX							
1	2	3	4	5	6	7	8
H	B	A	C	T	D	M	F

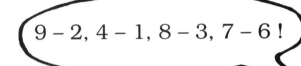

$9 - 2, 4 - 1, 8 - 3, 7 - 6$!

$$\begin{array}{r} 9 \\ -2 \\ \hline \end{array} \qquad \begin{array}{r} 4 \\ -1 \\ \hline \end{array} \qquad \begin{array}{r} 8 \\ -3 \\ \hline \end{array} \qquad \begin{array}{r} 7 \\ -6 \\ \hline \end{array}$$

HELP BOX: When you take one number away from another number to get an amount, it is called **subtraction**. The picture symbol used for subtraction is called a **minus sign (–)**. The amount left over is called the **difference**.

Skills: 1-digit subtraction, problem solving

NIKKI'S GRADE BOOSTER CHALLENGE

Nikki the Night Owl has been working on her homework for so long that she is confusing her numbers with her letters! To help Nikki, look at her subtraction problems below. Can you figure out what numbers the letters should be? Write the answers on the blank lines. If you need help with subtraction, look at the help box at the bottom of the page.

98	B3	12
− 17	− 10	− 5
A1	33	C

75	E7	2F
− D	− 13	− 5
70	24	21

A = ___   B = ___   C = ___

D = ___   E = ___   F = ___

HELP BOX: How to subtract **2-digit numbers:**
1. Subtract the numbers in the ones' place.
2. If you are subtracting a larger number from a smaller number, borrow 1 ten for 10 ones.
3. Subtract the numbers in the tens' place.
4. Write the difference, or the amount left over.

$$\begin{array}{r} {}^{1}\!2\;{}^{1}5 \\ -\;0\;7 \\ \hline 1\;8 \end{array}$$

JENN IN THE JUNGLE

Jenn lives in a jungle in a warm country. Jenn loves her country because it is full of animals. She has created the puzzle below so you can find out what her country's flag looks like. Solve each of the subtraction problems. Then follow the directions to color in the flag with crayons.

Color the sections with answers between 1 and 25 green.

Color the sections with answers between 26 and 50 yellow.

Color the sections with answers between 51 and 75 black.

Color the sections with answers between 76 and 99 blue.

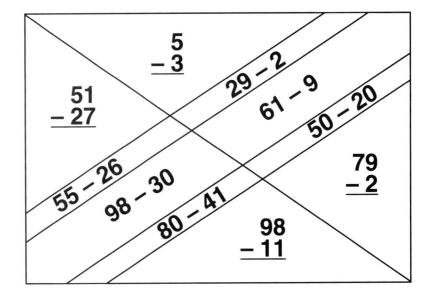

Problems shown in the puzzle:

$$5 - 3$$

$$29 - 2$$

$$61 - 9$$

$$50 - 20$$

$$51 - 27$$

$$55 - 26$$

$$98 - 30$$

$$80 - 41$$

$$79 - 2$$

$$98 - 11$$

GRADE BOOSTER!

2

Use an atlas or an encyclopedia to answer these questions: What country does this flag represent? What continent is it on? What is that country's capital?

Skills: 1- and 2-digit subtraction, deduction

SUBWAY SUBTRACTION

Look at the people on the subway train below. How many people are there? When you have counted them, read the questions and write the answers in the space provided.

The train is about to stop at Piccadilly Circus. It's a popular stop and 6 people get off. How many are left on the train after it pulls away from Piccadilly Circus?

_____

If the train goes on to make a stop at Van Ness and 1 person gets off, how many people will be left on the train? _____

If the train breaks down after it leaves Van Ness and the conductor needs 6 people to get out and push it to the next stop, will he have enough people? _____

Skills: 1- and 2-digit subtraction, borrowing tens

SHOPPING SPREE

Colin, Trevor, and Dylan mowed lawns all summer to earn money. They are at the toy store with their money. Read about each boy, and then choose the toy that he wants and can afford to buy. If you need help with subtraction, look at the help box at the bottom of the next page.

Skills: 3-digit subtraction, borrowing tens and hundreds, deduction, classification

Colin has earned $200. He wants something to use in the snow. What can he buy? _____ How much money will he have left? _____

Trevor has earned $250. He wants something with wheels. What can he buy? _____ How much money will he have left?

_____

Dylan has earned $180. He wants something with buttons to push. What can he buy? _____
How much money will he have left? _____

HELP BOX: How to subtract **3-digit numbers:**
1. Subtract the numbers in the ones' place.
2. If you are subtracting a larger number from a smaller number, borrow 1 ten for 10 ones.
3. Subtract the numbers in the tens' place.
4. If you are subtracting a larger number from a smaller number, borrow 1 hundred for 10 tens.
5. Subtract the numbers in the hundreds' place.

Skills: 3-digit subtraction, borrowing tens and hundreds, deduction, classification

LET'S REVIEW: SUBTRACTION

Look at the steps below. Solve all the problems in each of the steps. Then use crayons to color in the box that contains a problem that has a different answer than the others in that step.

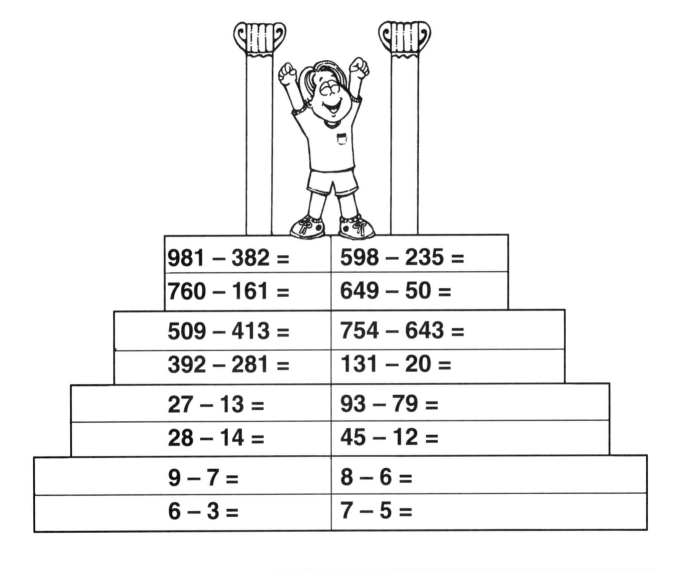

981 – 382 =	598 – 235 =
760 – 161 =	649 – 50 =
509 – 413 =	754 – 643 =
392 – 281 =	131 – 20 =
27 – 13 =	93 – 79 =
28 – 14 =	45 – 12 =
9 – 7 =	8 – 6 =
6 – 3 =	7 – 5 =

TOGETHER TIME: With an adult friend, take turns measuring each other's hair with a ruler. Whose hair is longer? By how much? Use subtraction to find out. Do the same for each other's arms, legs, and fingers.

Skills: 1-, 2-, and 3-digit subtraction with borrowing

AWARD
CERTIFICATE

_____

(my name)

Is SUPER at Subtraction!

CODE FUN

Farmer Becky likes to tell corny jokes. She has a joke for you. To find the answer, solve all the **multiplication** problems. Then match each answer to a letter using the code breaker. If you need help with multiplication, look at the help box at the bottom of the page.

Why is 6 afraid of 7?

CODE BREAKER						
56	72	49	35	16	100	81
N	V	S	E	T	A	I

Answer: Because . . .

```
  7    7    8    5    8      10   8    5       7    9    8    7
 x7   x5   x9   x7   x7     x10  x2   x7      x8   x9   x7   x5
```

HELP BOX: When we **multiply,** we are actually adding two or more numbers together. The numbers we multiply are called **factors**. The picture symbol for multiplication is a **times sign (x)**. The answer to a multiplication problem is called a **product**.

For example: + + = 6 pears **or** 3 x 2 = 6

Skills: multiplication, problem solving

BAKING BROWNIES

Maria's brownies are so popular that when she bakes them, she has to **double** the recipe. To double something means to multiply it by 2. On the lines below, write the amount of each ingredient you have to use when you double the recipe.

Recipe:

2 cups of flour

1 cup of cocoa

3 eggs

1 stick of butter

When you double the recipe, you will need:

____ cups of flour

____ cups of cocoa

____ eggs

____ sticks of butter

Now you can make twice as many brownies!

TOGETHER TIME: With an adult friend, find an actual recipe for brownies in a cookbook. Then double the recipe to make a big batch of brownies!

Skills: practical applications of multiplication, measuring

285

HAND PLAY

Trace your hands in the space below. You know how many fingers you have without even counting. But can you show how many fingers you have using a multiplication equation? Try it on the next page.

Skills: multiplication, fine motor skills

How many fingers do you have on each hand? Write that number in the box below.

What sign (× or +) would you put on the line between the boxes to form an equation?

How many hands do you have? Write that number in the box below.

☐

_____

☐

Now write the answer on the line after the equals (=) sign!

= _____

GRADE BOOSTER!

From left to right, number each of your fingers on your drawing. Use crayons to color the odd-numbered fingers green and the even-numbered fingers blue.

Skills: multiplication, fine motor skills

BUILDING AIRPLANES

Pretend you own your own airline. It's called _____
_____ Air.   (my name)

Business is doing so well that
you have to build 5 new
airplanes! To build the new
planes, you need to buy the
parts. Use multiplication in
the problems below to find out
how many of each part you need to buy. Then circle all
the factors and draw a triangle around the products.

How many jet engines do you need?

1   ×   **5**   = _____ jet engines

(for each airplane)   (number of airplanes)

How many wings do you need?

2   ×   **5**   = _____ wings

(for each airplane)   (number of airplanes)

How many landing tires do you need?

10   ×   **5**   = _____ tires

(for each airplane)   (number of airplanes)

On a separate piece of paper, draw a picture of one of
the newly built airplanes in your fleet. Be sure to
include your own logo, or design, on the plane.

Skills: multiplication

WHAT IS THE COUNTRY?

Karl lives in a country far away. His country has big cities, but it also has castles and thick, dark forests. The puzzle below will show you the flag for Karl's country. Solve the multiplication problems in the puzzle. Then follow the directions to color in the flag with crayons.

Color the area with a product of 56 red.

Color the area with a product of 45 black.

Color the area with a product of 24 orange.

5 × 9
7 × 8
6 × 4

GRADE BOOSTER!

Use an atlas or an encyclopedia to answer these questions: What country does this flag represent? What continent is it on? What is this country's capital? What other countries are on the same continent?

Skills: multiplication

LET'S REVIEW: MULTIPLICATION

Can you find your way through the maze of multiplication products below? Solve each of the multiplication problems, then use your answers to guide you through the maze. The answers are in the order you must follow to get through the maze.

1. **3 × 4 =** _____   2. **7 × 9 =** _____   3. **6 × 3 =** _____

4. **7 × 8 =** _____   5. **6 × 7 =** _____   6. **9 × 9 =** _____

7. **5 × 5 =** _____   8. **10 × 3 =** _____

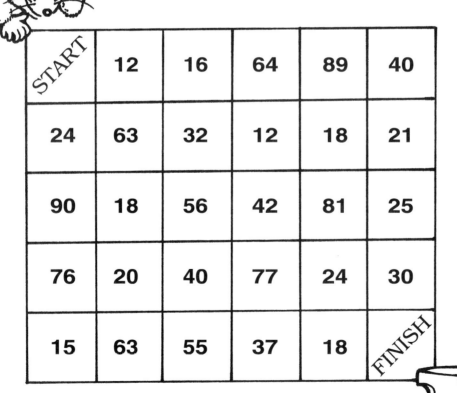

START	12	16	64	89	40
24	63	32	12	18	21
90	18	56	42	81	25
76	20	40	77	24	30
15	63	55	37	18	FINISH

Skills: multiplication

Congratulations!

HURRAY!

_____
(my name)

**Is Unequaled When It
Comes to
Multiplication!**

LOOK CLOSELY!

Roberto has cut his daughter Sierra's birthday cake into **equal parts**. Each equal part is called a **fraction**. For fun, Roberto made the puzzle below for the guests at his daughter's birthday party.

Look closely at the small box containing four fractions.

½	⅓
¼	⅙

Now look at the large box containing many fractions. Find where the small box is hidden in the large box and draw a line around it.

½	⅓	⅙	½	⅓
⅙	¼	½	⅓	⅙
½	⅓	¼	⅙	¼
¼	⅕	½	⅓	⅙

Now write out all the fractions in words:

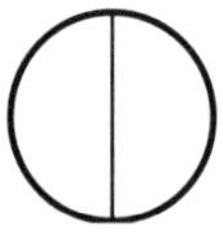

½ = _____

⅓ = _____

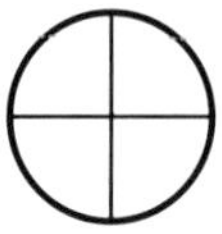

¼ = _____

⅕ = _____

⅙ = _____

Skills: identifying fractions in numbers and words

BAKERY BINGE

Look at the bakery items below. Use crayons to color in a fraction, or part, of each item or group of items as directed. Then write the fraction in numbers next to each item or group.

Color one-fifth.

Color one-third.

Color one-fourth.

Color one-sixth.

TOGETHER TIME: Go to a bakery or a grocery store with an adult friend. Pick out a pie and bring it home. When it is time for dessert, let your friend decide how many pieces to cut the pie into. Then, with your friend nearby, cut the pie into equal pieces, or fractions. When you are serving the pie, tell your family or guests what fraction of the pie you are serving them.

Skills: identifying fractions in words and numbers

LET'S REVIEW: FRACTIONS

Look at the planets in outer space below. Match each planet with the fraction that tells what part of the planet is shaded. Draw a line from each planet to the correct fraction.

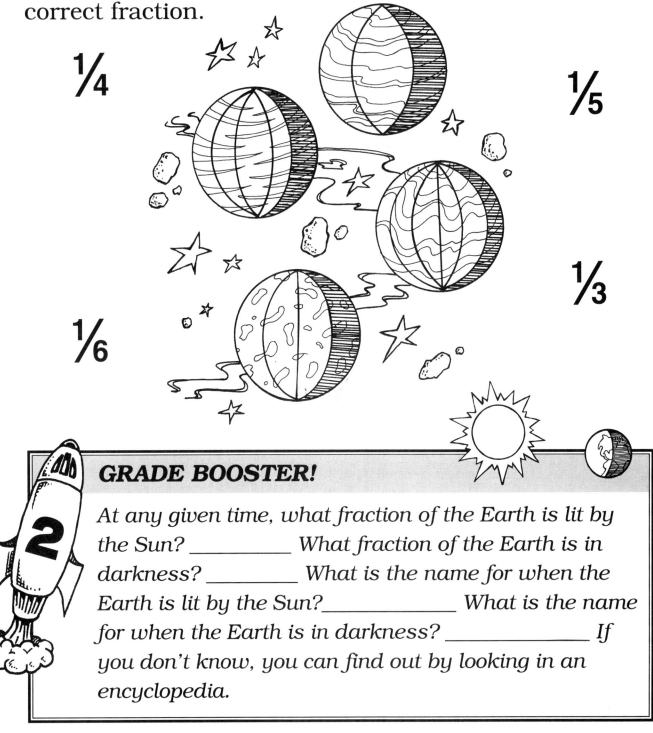

¼

⅕

⅓

⅙

GRADE BOOSTER!

At any given time, what fraction of the Earth is lit by the Sun? _____ What fraction of the Earth is in darkness? _____ What is the name for when the Earth is lit by the Sun?_____ What is the name for when the Earth is in darkness? _____ If you don't know, you can find out by looking in an encyclopedia.

Skills: identifying fractions, critical thinking

YOU'RE FAR OUT!

_____

(my name)

Is Out of This World When It Comes to Fractions!

Addition, Subtraction, Multiplication

MATH FOR TWO

Play this game with an adult friend. All you need to
know is how to add, subtract, multiply, and have fun!
Oh, and you'll need a penny, too. On the next page is a
game board with many problems to solve. Below are two
game cards, one for you and one for your adult friend.
Decide who will go first. The first person starts the game
by tossing the penny up so that it lands on the game
board. That person now has to solve the problem on
which the penny landed. When a player gets an answer
right, he or she should color it on the game card. Take
turns until one of the game cards is filled!

Your Game Card

25	101
36	77
233	82
365	50

Friend's Game Card

25	101
36	77
233	82
365	50

Skills: addition, subtraction, multiplication

$4 \times 9 =$ _____

$27 + 23 =$ _____

The number after
100: _____

$467 - 234 =$ _____

$33 + 44 =$ _____

The next number
in the series:

5, 10, 15, 20,

_____

$147 + 218 =$ _____

$100 - 18 =$ _____

CRACK THE CODE!

Lisa loves to watch horse races. Solve each of the problems below, then match each answer to the correct letter in the code breaker. Write the letters in the blank boxes to help Lisa find the answer to her question about horse races.

CODE BREAKER											
129	120	78	71	2	61	28	49	40	54	30	56
W	O	H	S	N	I	W	E	C	A	L	P

$$
\begin{array}{r} 39 \\ -11 \end{array}
\quad
\begin{array}{r} 88 \\ -27 \end{array}
\quad
\begin{array}{r} 42 \\ -40 \end{array}
$$

What do you call first, second, and third place in a horse race?

$$
\begin{array}{r} 7 \\ \times 8 \end{array}
\quad
\begin{array}{r} 5 \\ \times 6 \end{array}
\quad
\begin{array}{r} 6 \\ \times 9 \end{array}
\quad
\begin{array}{r} 8 \\ \times 5 \end{array}
\quad
\begin{array}{r} 7 \\ \times 7 \end{array}
$$

$$
\begin{array}{r} 59 \\ +12 \end{array}
\quad
\begin{array}{r} 33 \\ +45 \end{array}
\quad
\begin{array}{r} 61 \\ +59 \end{array}
\quad
\begin{array}{r} 67 \\ +62 \end{array}
$$

Skills: addition, subtraction, multiplication, problem solving

AMOS THE ALIEN

Amos the Alien looks a lot different from you! Look at the different number of arms, legs, fingers, and toes he has. Then answer the questions below.

How many fingers does Amos have in all? _____

Hint: Multiply the number of hands Amos has by the number of fingers on each hand.

How many more fingers does Amos have than you have? _____

Hint: To find the answer, use subtraction.

If Amos and his twin brother were buying shoes together, how many shoes would they need in all? _____

Hint: To find the answer, use addition or multiplication.

How many more antennae does Amos have than you have? _____

Hint: To find the answer, use subtraction.

GRADE BOOSTER!

Amos likes to hop instead of walk. Each time he hops he makes 3 footprints. If Amos hops 6 times, how many footprints will he make? _____

BERRY PATCH

Tony and Morgan were out picking strawberries when they decided to play a game. They wrote equations but left out the math symbols. **Math symbols** are plus signs (+), minus signs (–), and multiplication signs (×). Help them figure out the missing symbol for each equation.

Hint: To get started, try one of the symbols and see if it works. Continue with different symbols until you find one that gives you the same answer as the one in the equation.

Choose one symbol (+, –, ×) to make the equation correct.

$$3 \boxed{} 6 = 18$$

$$20 \boxed{} 3 = 17$$

$$3 \boxed{} 7 = 21$$

$$200 \boxed{} 150 = 50$$

$$346 \boxed{} 79 = 425$$

GRADE BOOSTER!

What about 2 $\boxed{}$ 2 = 4? Does that equation have one math symbol that fits or more than one? _____
Why? _____

Skills: addition, subtraction, multiplication, critical thinking

LUCKY SAND DOLLARS

Which sand dollar on the beach contains all the answers to the problems below? Solve the problems, then use a crayon to color in the correct sand dollar.

$$126 + 321 = \underline{\hspace{3cm}}$$

$$97 - 66 = \underline{\hspace{3cm}}$$

$$3 \times 5 = \underline{\hspace{3cm}}$$

$$27 - 18 = \underline{\hspace{3cm}}$$

What number has a 3 in the hundreds' place, a 7 in the tens' place, and a 1 in the ones' place? \underline{\hspace{3cm}}

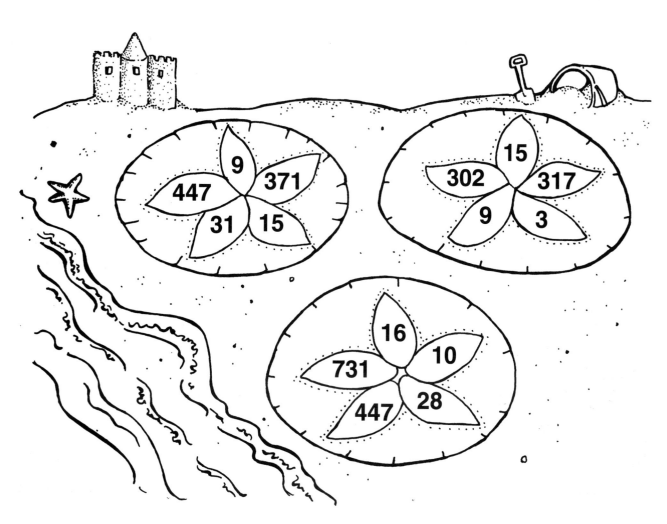

BICYCLE POWER

Pedal to success! Solve each of the equations in the bicycle wheels below. Then use a crayon to color in the part of each wheel that has a different answer from the other parts of that wheel.

$$\begin{array}{r} 9 \\ -\ 4 \\ \hline \end{array}$$

$$\begin{array}{r} 9 \\ \times\ 4 \\ \hline \end{array}$$

$$\begin{array}{r} 236 \\ +\ 1 \\ \hline \end{array}$$

$$\begin{array}{r} 9 \\ \times\ 9 \\ \hline \end{array}$$

$$\begin{array}{r} 18 \\ +\ 18 \\ \hline \end{array}$$

$$\begin{array}{r} 73 \\ -\ 37 \\ \hline \end{array}$$

$$\begin{array}{r} 729 \\ -\ 492 \\ \hline \end{array}$$

$$\begin{array}{r} 106 \\ +\ 131 \\ \hline \end{array}$$

GRADE BOOSTER!

If you got a new bicycle that had 25 spokes on each wheel, how many spokes would the bicycle have in all?

_____ (+, −, or x) _____ = _____

Skills: 2- and 3-digit addition, subtraction, multiplication, deduction

YOU'RE ON YOUR WAY!

_____

(my name)

Has a Ticket on the Math Steamship and Is Ready to Cruise Into Third Grade Math!

Answers

ANSWERS

Page 12
My friend is coming today. **W**e are going to play tag. **T**hen we are going to catch flies. **I**t will be fun!
GB: *Parent:* Stories will vary. Make sure each sentence begins with a capital letter.

Page 13
Peter, Russia
Ingrid, Sweden
Duncan, Scotland
Keiko, Japan
Jomo, Kenya
Maria, Mexico
Sentences will vary.

Page 14
1. Hillside Park
2. Center Street
3. Lou's Market
4. Center Library
5. First Bank
6. Ace Garage
7. Best Bakery
TT: Answers will vary.

Page 15
Answers will vary.

Page 16
1. Fun in Space
2. All About Dogs
3. A Surprise at School
4. Real Heroes
5. Looking at Trees
Book titles and designs will vary.

Page 17
1. Dinosaurs lived millions of years ago.
2. How big were the largest dinosaurs?
3. Which dinosaur was the smallest?
4. Some dinosaurs had horns.
5. Dinosaurs hatched from eggs.
6. Many dinosaurs ate plants.
7. Did all dinosaurs have tails?
8. Why did the dinosaurs die out?
TT: Answers will vary.

Page 18
1. It is peaceful in the water.
2. Do you like to swim in the sea?
3. Watch out for that shark!
4. Is that an octopus?
5. Get out of the way!
6. Many animals live in the sea.
7. Look at the size of that whale!
8. Do all sea animals have scales?
GB: Sentences will vary.

Page 19
1. Nov.
2. Mrs.
3. Apr.
4. Dr.
5. Feb.
6. Mr.
7. Sept.
Rest of answer will vary.

Page 20
1. My dog's name is Flip.
2. Look how cute he is!
3. His birthday is Mar. 4.
4. Can you come to his party on Friday?
Parent: Sentence should tell about a pet. It should begin with a capital letter and end with appropriate punctuation.

Page 22
circuses	whistles
glasses	bunches
clowns	cages
boxes	sandwiches
tents	bushes
dishes	wagons

TT: Results will vary.

Page 23
stories	days
buggies	cities
trays	pennies
keys	berries
ponies	monkeys
hobbies	families
valleys	donkeys

Page 24
men
sheep
fish
oxen
feet
women
teeth
geese
children
moose
GB: Sentences will vary.

Page 25
1. brush**e**s
2. b**u**ses
3. **t**oys
4. app**l**es
5. **f**oxes
6. d**r**esses
7. m**e**n.
8. famil**i**es
9. tee**t**h
10. **s**heep
11. **b**enches

$$b\ u\ t\ t\ e\ r\ f\ l\ i\ e\ s$$
11 2 3 9 7 6 5 4 8 1 10

Page 26
is not – isn't
are not – aren't
has not – hasn't
was not – wasn't
have not – haven't
did not – didn't
could not – couldn't
will not – won't
TT: Sentences will vary.

Page 27

Hi, Grandpa!

It's going to be fun visiting you at your cabin. Mom said **she's** going to write you a letter today. Mom and Dad are so busy that **they're** both happy to go on vacation. Dad said **he's** going to take me fishing with him. **I'm** so excited I can't sleep! I hope **you're** excited about seeing us, too! **We're** all looking forward to the trip. See you soon!

Love,

Jeff

Page 28

1. I'll
2. He'll
3. They've
4. You'll
5. We've
6. she'll
7. I've
8. he'll

GB: Sentences will vary.

Page 29

do not – don't

is not – isn't

it is – it's

he is – he's

she will – she'll

you are – you're

they have – they've

will not – won't

I'm – I am

she's – she is

we're – we are

aren't – are not

hasn't – has not

they're – they are

we'll – we will

couldn't – could not

Page 30

1. Jodi	1. Evan
2. Kyle	2. Hans
3. Meg	3. Rob
4. Pam	4. Sue

1. Bob	1. Fred
2. Greg	2. Lynn
3. Teri	3. Ned
4. Will	4. Val

GB: *Parent:* Make sure names are listed in alphabetical order.

Page 31

1. happy	1. field
2. hive	2. flower
3. honey	3. food
4. hurry	4. fresh

1. smooth	1. pick
2. sticky	2. plant
3. sweet	3. pollen
4. syrup	4. pretty

Page 32

1. A big lion roared.
2. Four giraffes munched quietly.
3. A bear climbed on rocks.
4. People saw several snakes.
5. A child fed some squirrels.
6. Elephants raised their trunks.
7. A group of seals swam.

Page 34

unhappy, unlock, untie

disobey, dislike, dishonest

1. unhappy
2. untie
3. dishonest
4. unlock
5. disobey
6. dislike

Sentences will vary.

Page 35

1. reheat
2. repaint
3. rebuild
4. rewrap
5. replant
6. rewrite
7. repack
8. reread

GB: Sentences will vary.

Page 36

1. painful
2. painless
3. useful
4. useless
5. fearless
6. fearful
7. colorless
8. colorful
9. helpful
10. helpless

Page 37

These words should be circled in the story: brightly, slowly, Suddenly, happily, quietly, loudly

1. slowly
2. happily
3. brightly
4. loudly
5. Suddenly
6. quietly

GB: Words will vary.

Page 38

red – disappear, refill

blue – hopeful, neatly

yellow – unsafely, dishonestly

1. unsafely
2. hopeful
3. neatly
4. disappear
5. refill
6. dishonestly

Page 39

1. throw, toss
2. jump, leap
3. shout, cheer
4. strong, mighty
5. prize, award
6. exciting, thrilling

Answers

Page 40
old – new
big – little
loud – quiet
begin – end
front – back
empty – full
always – never
under – over
strong – weak
GB: Sentences will vary.

Page 41
1. write, right
2. one, won
3. week, weak
4. ate, eight
5. knew, new
6. four, for
7. our, hour

Page 42
scared, afraid – S
start, begin – S
write, right – H
pretty, lovely – S
hard, soft – A
full, empty – A
front, back – A
new, knew – H
ate, eight – H

Page 44
Answers will vary.

Page 45
month – June
girl – Wendy
state – Texas
boy – Eric
dog – Wags
city – Boston
holiday – Easter
planet – Jupiter

Page 46
wiggle
glide
hop
slide
hoot
soar
trot
roar
Pictures will vary.

Page 47
1. rides
2. drive
3. checks
4. visits
5. play
6. drinks
7. practice
8. cleans
GB: Sentences will vary.

Page 48
1. traveled
2. unpacked
3. hiked
4. rowed
5. waded
6. explored
7. decided
8. enjoyed
GB: Words will vary.

Page 49

Page 50
furry rabbit
grassy field
smooth pebble
leafy tree
deep river
prickly porcupine
wooden cabin
scaly snake
Sentences will vary.

Page 51
1. strange
2. friendly
3. gigantic
4. long
5. amazing
6. sleek
7. surprised
8. cold
GB: Sentences will vary.

Page 52
Alex – red
cup – blue
big – green
bank – blue
read – yellow
Mexico – red
funny – green
teacher – blue
throw – yellow
soft – green
write – yellow
April – red
heavy – green
tiptoe – yellow
river – blue
Friday – red
shiny – green
Kim – red
climb – yellow
house – blue

Page 54
1. yes
2. no
3. yes
4. no
5. no
6. yes
7. no
8. yes

Page 55
1. A boy
2. The beach umbrella
3. Seagulls
4. Many people
5. A girl
6. A sailboat
Sentences will vary.

Page 56
1. takes piano lessons
2. is a good guitar player
3. plays the flute
4. is a stringed instrument
5. beat their drums
6. has black and white keys

The trumpet is made of brass.
The music teacher waved a baton.
The school band meets every
Friday.

Page 57

Jake is behind Tina.
The girl hits the ball.
The dog sees a baby.
The cat is under the table.

Page 58

1. Is the sky gray?
2. Are there puddles everywhere?
3. Are the children wearing raincoats?
4. Is a boy carrying an umbrella?
GB: Sentences will vary.

Page 59

Parent: Various combinations may be used as long as the sentences are complete and make sense.
Here are some suggestions:
1. We have one dog and two cats.
2. The truck is shiny and red.
3. Maria went shopping and she bought a coat.
4. The house is old and needs repairs.
5. Antonio likes horses and Diana likes turtles.

Page 60

1. soared
2. glided
3. screeched
4. darted
5. flapped
6. strutted
7. cooed
8. sipped

Page 61

Parent: Sentences will vary, but they should describe the pictures appropriately and include descriptive words.

Page 62

Monica packed her suitcase. She went to the airport. Monica got on the plane.

Jamal washed his shirt. He put the shirt into the dryer. Jamal hung the shirt in his closet.

Page 63

Answers and stories will vary.

Page 64

The big cat is sleeping. – yes
The clown puppet in the box. – no

(The leaves) fell slowly to the ground.
(Some children) played on the swings.
(A duck) swam in the pond.

Is the car in the garage?
Are there coins on the table?

Sue bought some corn and some carrots.

Page 70

B S W K M
G C Z P Q
L T D N W
V X R F H
GB: J and Y are not pictured. Rest of answer will vary.

Page 71

long ā words: rain, baby, rake, tail
long ē words: bee, feet, pea, seal
long ī words: slide, fire, kite, child

Page 72

long ō words: soap, toe, bone, note
long ū words: music, fruit, cute, juice
y as in long ē: happy, baby, puppy, crazy, funny, sleepy, lucky, silly
y as in long ī: my, sky, by, cry, dry, try

Page 73

short ă words: cat, pan, man
short ĕ words: nest, bed, tent
short ĭ words: pin, mitten, swim
Eel, kite, and *airplane* all have long vowel sounds.

Page 74

short ŏ words: box, doll, octopus
short ŭ words: sun, nut, skunk
Boot and *toe* have long vowel sounds.
GB: Answers will vary.

Page 75

red long vowel words: cane, key, slide, cube, rain, baby, smoke, puppy
blue short vowel words: mop, puppy, cat, jet, skunk
Puppy has both a short and a long vowel sound.

Page 76

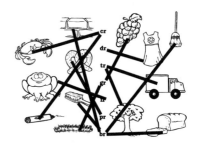

GB: br has the most words: 4
pr, fr, and **dr** have the least words: 1 each

Page 77

(C)larice the (C)lown needs (g)lasses to see (c)learly through the (c)louds.
blanket, blocks, clock, flag, flower, glasses, plane, sleep, slide
GB: Answers will vary.

Answers

Page 78

Page 79

(Chucky) the (Chipmunk) (chuckled) and (shrieked) (when) he got his (shoe) caught in the (wheel).

wh: whiskers
th: throat, thumb
ch: cheese, cherry
sh: shell, shoe
GB: Answers will vary.

Page 80

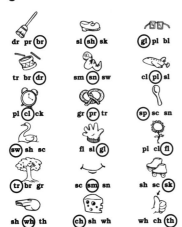

Page 82

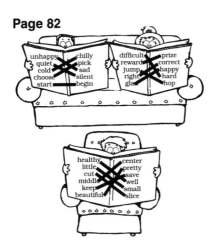

Page 83

little, car, finish, rush, shout, quick
TT: Answers will vary but may include: exam: test; large: big or huge; maybe: possibly; choose: pick; scared: frightened; friend: companion; fall: autumn; high: tall.

Page 84

easy: hard; fast: slow; short: tall; loud: quiet; hot: cold; play: work; night: day; right: wrong; in: out; empty: full

Page 85

Answers will vary but may include: closes, clean, far, on, and small.

Page 86

GB: There are 7 sets of synonyms and 8 sets of antonyms. One set of words is homonyms.

Page 87

two: to; blew: blue; knot: not; meat: meet; mail: male; weigh: way; sum: some; heal: heel; know: no; sew: so; whole: hole; hear: here; rode: road; right: write; sale: sail; tale: tail

Page 88

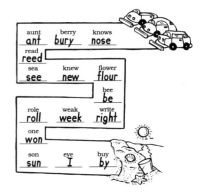

Page 89

Hal the (horse) has had a (sore) throat all (week) His voice has been (hoarse) and (weak) So instead of running around the fields, he has been lounging on the grass watching the birds (soar) through the sky.

3 pairs of homonyms
pears, OK, OK, piece, weigh, OK

Page 90

day, ugly, middle, white, berry, nose, weak, hole, right, one, kid, hot

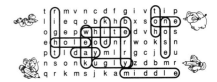

Page 92

popcorn, rainbow, backyard, cupcake, toothbrush, bookcase, bluebird, sunshine, newspaper, sidewalk, suitcase, afternoon
GB: Answers will vary.

Page 93

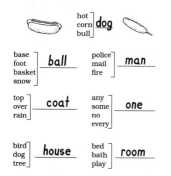

hot corn bull → *dog*

base foot basket snow → *ball*

police mail fire → *man*

top over rain → *coat*

any some no every → *one*

bird dog tree → *house*

bed bath play → *room*

TT: *Parent:* Make sure answer reflects child's knowledge of how to alphabetize correctly.

Page 94

Answers will vary.
GB: Answers will vary but may include: ham: lamb, dam, ram; mitt: hit, bit, kit.

Page 95

trees, apples, bikes, balloons
ladies, candies, flies, families

Page 96

buses, boxes, sandwiches, fishes

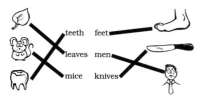

teeth — feet
leaves — men
mice — knives

Page 97

don't, it's, you'll, isn't, wouldn't
I am, could not, she will, that is, has not, was not
GB: Answers will vary.

Page 98

On Sunday morning, Jamie and her family were going to the zoo. Jamie couldn't wait. She hadn't been to the zoo before and she knew she'd love it. Her big brother Jeffrey told Jamie, it's so much fun! You'll love the monkeys. They're so cute."

Jamie had a great time at the zoo. She didn't want to leave when the day was over. So her parents told her they'd be able to come back soon.

couldn't	could not
hadn't	had not
she'd	she would
It's	It is
You'll	You will
They're	They are
didn't	did not
they'd	they would

Page 99

One-syllable words: sleep, soap, laugh, rain, school, house, bear
Two-syllable words: flower, spelling, popcorn, candy, bubbles, funny
Three-syllable words: different, remember, basketball, grandmother
TT: Answers will vary.

Page 100

1: girl, grape, gum, milk
2: bathtub, mailman, student, teacher
3: history, professor, volleyball
GB: See order above. Operator has four syllables.

Page 101

sandwiches, can't, popcorn, one, butterfly, four, don't, family
TT: Answers will vary.

Page 103

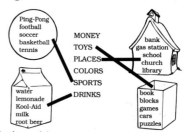

Ping-Pong football soccer basketball tennis

MONEY
TOYS
PLACES
COLORS
SPORTS
DRINKS

bank gas station school church library

water lemonade Kool-Aid milk root beer

book blocks games cars puzzles

fruits, girls, states, seasons, round

Page 104

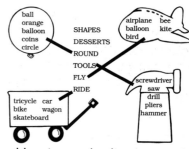

ball orange balloon coins circle

SHAPES
DESSERTS
ROUND
TOOLS
FLY
RIDE

airplane balloon bird — bee kite

tricycle car bike wagon skateboard

screwdriver saw drill pliers hammer

cold, pets or animals, green, pets or animals, vegetables

Page 105

January, February, March, April, May, June, July, August, September, October, November, December
GB: Monday, Tuesday, Wednesday, Thursday, Friday, Saturday, Sunday

Page 106

Parent: Make sure child's additions reflect his or her understanding of the text.

Page 107

Parent: Make sure child's additions reflect his or her understanding of the text.

Answers

Page 108

Page 109

TT: Answers will vary.

Page 110

- The ball is round. _F_
- That is a cute dog. _O_
- Mom works every day. _F_
- Pizza tastes good. _O_
- Playing at the park is fun. _O_
- The car has a radio. _F_
- Flowers smell good. _O_
- The music is too loud. _O_
- Laurie and Suzie are friends. _F_

GB: Answers will vary.

Page 111

Parent: Make sure child's sentences reflect his or her understanding of the text.

Page 112

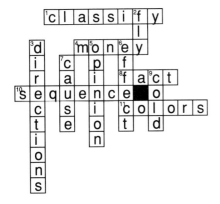

Page 114

Chrissi's dad is a policeman.
Many things are green.
I enjoy music.

Page 115

GB: When you eat an orange, you use your sense of touch, taste, smell, and sight.
When you watch a movie, you use your sense of sight and hearing.

Page 116

c: he was storing them for the winter.
d: fall.
c: have lots to eat.

Page 117

c: bike
b: help
a: cookies
a: grandmother's

Page 118

My name is *Carlos*. I am a *car*. I am just a few years *old*. My paint color is *white*. My seats are as *green* as the grass. I hold *two* people.

In the morning my engine is *cold* from sitting outside all *night*. To start my motor, Carl puts his *key* in the car and turns it on. He steps on the *gas*. I start to move, but not too quickly. I'm still not quite *awake*. Soon I can go really *fast*.

Page 119

Carolyn has a pet cat.
It lives in her apartment.
It eats cat food.
Carolyn plays with the cat.

The family got a new car.
The car is maroon.
There are five seat belts.
The seats are black.

Page 120

Pamela had a birthday party.
The party was at the park.
Eight friends came to the party.
They ate pizza and birthday cake.
Pamela is seven years old.
Rest of answers will vary.
TT: Answers will vary.

Page 121

Answers will vary.
Parent: Answers should reflect child's understanding of the paragraph.
GB: Answers will vary.

Page 122

They left to go camping early in the morning.
Their dad went to the ranger station to register.
Ken and Dave set up the tent.
Tom unrolled the sleeping bags inside the tent.
They went to Sequoia National Park.
Rest of answers will vary.

Page 128

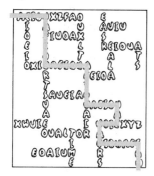

GB: Sample answers–sky, cry, dry, hymn, fly, by, my, spy, why. Rest of answer will vary.

Page 129

Yellow triangles should form a star. Shapes colored yellow contain the words **if**, **red**, **cat**, **dog**, **raft**, and **run**. They all have short vowel sounds. All the other triangles should be colored blue because they contain long vowel words.

GB: Astronomy is the study of stars and planets. You can find out by using a dictionary.

Page 130

1=C, 2=O, 3=P, 4=S
Answer to riddle: triceracops.

Page 131

Answers will vary but may include:
Eric, Ernest
umbrella, uncle, ukulele
jelly, jar, jug, jam
thick, thin, tough
walk, wade, worry

Page 132

Answer to riddle: starfish.

Page 133

Page 135

Parent: Child should color cookies with the following synonym pairs brown–happy, glad; hard, difficult; center, middle; slim, skinny; big, large; fix, repair; nice, kind; smooth, slick; small, little; and spicy, hot.

GB: Cookies containing the following pairs of antonyms should be colored yellow–mend, rip; awake, asleep.

Page 136

Answers will vary but may include:
large–big, huge, gigantic, colossal
soar–fly, coast, cruise
curved–rounded, bow-shaped
tiny–small, miniature, dwarflike

GB: Brontosaurus, Pterodactyl, Stegosaurus, and Tyrannosaurus rex.

Page 137

Page 138

Evan is a small boy who rides a big bike at the motocross races. He rides with his friends. Some of them are old and some are young. Some go very fast and some go very slow. They all have fun. Evan's bike is new. He likes it better than his old one. The races are usually held during the day, but sometimes they are held at night under the big lights. At the races, Evan's dad shouts "Go, Evan, go!" At bedtime, his dad whispers, "Good night, Evan, good night."

Parent: Make sure child circles each pair of antonyms in a different color.

Page 139

threw, sea, two, herd, would, sleigh, horse
Answer to riddle: wal-rust.

Page 140

Parent: Child should color the area with the following pairs of homonyms yellow–sew, so; two, to; one, won; sun, son; ate, eight; and berry, bury. All other areas should be colored green.
Sidney caught a flower in his web. A homonym for **flower** is **flour**.

Page 141

Garage is from France.
Kindergarten is from Germany.
Burrito is from Mexico.
Parent: Child should draw lines matching these items.
TT: France–French fries, French toast, berets (hats), crepes; Germany–pretzels, strudel, Beethoven's music; Mexico–nachos, salsa, tortillas, churros, Mexican hat dance, ponchos.

Pages 142–143

Asia wins.

TT: Sample answers—pollution and destruction of their homes or habitat, being hunted, the extermination or destruction of their food supply, and disease.

Answers

Pages 144–145

Rest of answer will vary.

Pages 146–147

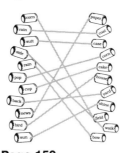

Anemic means lacking in red blood cells.

Scurvy is a disease caused by a lack of vitamin C.

Rest of answer will vary.

Page 148

Parent: Make sure child draws a line connecting each word to its associated scene.

A homonym for **weather** is **whether**.

Sample antonyms for **sunny** are **rainy**, **cloudy**, and **foggy**.

Sample synonyms for **cold** are **chilly**, **freezing**, and **cool**.

Sample words that rhyme with **cold** are **bold**, **fold**, and **hold**.

Rest of answer will vary.

An umbrella appears in two different scenes, once to keep off rain and once to keep off sun. In both cases, it acts as a shield and protects the person.

Page 150

Max the mouse loved to sing. He liked it better than baseball or basketball. Almost everyone thought Max had a beautiful voice—everyone except his next-door neighbor. One wintry night Max was in his backyard singing in the moonlight when his neighbor threw a snowball at him. Then he yelled, "Please stop singing, Max. Your voice sounds like a cowbell and it is giving me a toothache! If you come inside I'll make you some popcorn!" Now, Max liked popcorn even better than singing, so he stopped singing and went inside.

There are ten compound words.

Backyard comes first alphabetically.

Toothache comes last alphabetically.

GB: Answers will vary.

Page 151

Page 152

cat hat
nurse purse
pear chair
flame game
mouse blouse
TT: Answers will vary.

Page 153

Parent: Child should circle the following words in the story: **attack**, **back**, **crack**, **lack**, **pack**, **snack**, **track**, and **yak**.

GB: See alphabetical order above.

Page 154

chicks, books, lizards
mice, teeth, leaves
Rest of answer will vary.

Page 155

Parent: Child should circle these words in the story and place them in the following order–**couldn't**, **I'm**, **let's**, **weren't**, and **wouldn't**. Answer to riddle: two worms.

Pages 156–157

I'm stands for **I am**.
Isn't stands for **is not**.
We're stands for **we are**.
Shouldn't stands for **should not**.
You've stands for **you have**.

GB: The alphabet is the Greek alphabet used in the country of Greece.

A, **B**, **E**, **Z**, **X**, **H**, **I**, **K**, **M**, **N**, **O**, **P**, **T**, and **Y** are also found in the English alphabet. You can find this information in an encyclopedia or a book on the Greek language.

Page 158

Two-syllable words are **camel**, **snakeskin**, and **buzzard**. Child should color them red. Three-syllable words are **pyramid**, **oasis**, and **wonderful**. Child should color them brown.

A camel can go up to eight days without drinking water.

GB: Snakeskin is a compound word. It is made up of the words **snake** and **skin**.

Page 159

GB: Oliver eats the most foods at the party. Fred eats the least.
Parent: Make sure child chooses foods correctly.

Answers

Page 160

Page 162

GB: treasure

Page 163

Sample answers: birds, bears, tents, people camping, backpacks, campfires, deer, squirrels, and a forest ranger.

Page 164

a picture of a wing, yellow, one, raisin

Answers will vary for last item but may include the words **table**, **house**, **desk**, and **chair**.

TT: Pickles are made by soaking cucumbers in vinegar, spices, and brine, which is salty water. This mixture is also called pickling juice.

A grape is turned into a raisin by being dried in the sun or under heat. These processes are different in that the first is an acid-induced change, while the second is a heat-induced change. These processes are the same in that they both alter the original food.

Page 165

wood, crane, workmen

Parent: Child should circle **workmen** and put a star next to **crane**.

Pages 166–167

Answers will vary but may include:
Facts–Cheetahs can run 80 miles per hour. Leopards can climb trees. Tigers live in India. A group of lions is called a pride.
Opinions–Leopards are prettier than cheetahs. Lions are more gentle than cheetas and leopards.
Answer to question: morning.

Page 168

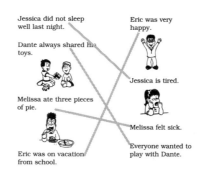

Page 169
CAUSE / EFFECT

Olaf had no fear of the whale / Olaf paddled closer to the whale.
Olaf paddled his kayak / Olaf's kayak moved through the water.
Olaf leaned over too far in his kayak / Olaf fell into the water.
The whale dove deep into the ocean / Olaf let go of the whale's fin.

Page 170

Things to do in the snow: ski, snowboard, and sled.
"Making snow people is fun!" and "Sledding is my favorite sport!" are opinions.
"No two snowflakes are exactly alike" is a fact.
Rest of answer will vary.

Page 172

spaceship, monkey, window, hungry, bed
Spaceships use fuel for power.
GB: Answers will vary.

Page 173

Answers will vary.

Page 174

Page 175

1. Once there was a piglet, which is a baby pig.
2. His friends all said, "You eat a lot."
3. He worried about what his friends said.
4. Then one day he read that piglets are supposed to eat a lot.
5. Then he was a happy piglet.
Rest of answer will vary.

Page 176

Laurie entered a watermelon-eating contest and won.
GB: Sample answers: water, melon, lemon, ram, lame, tame, late, lawn, meal, meat, raw, law, role, rate, teal, tale, trowel, tram, and tear.

313

Answers

Page 177

Page 178
Gus ate a flower, a mailbox, the books, and a chest of drawers.
Parent: Child should put a square around the flower and a triangle around the chest of drawers.

Page 179
House has a large red door, a chimney, a porch swing, yellow curtains, and a wishing well in the front yard.
GB: A chimney with smoke coming out of it.

Page 180
Color the airplane with three stripes on each wing, a dot on the tail, and two pilots in the cockpit.
TT: Answers will vary.

Page 181
Australia; sleeping; surprised, scared, or sad

Page 188

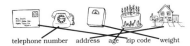

telephone number   address   age   zip code   weight

Page 189

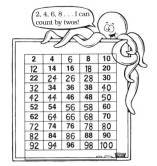

GB: All of the numbers are even.

Page 190
Parent: Make sure child spells numbers correctly.

Page 191
1-digit numbers: 7, 6, 8
2-digit numbers: 24, 35, 51, 49
3-digit numbers: 101, 120

Page 193

85	32	64
tens ones	tens ones	tens ones
8 5	3 2	6 4

71	90	45
tens ones	tens ones	tens ones
7 1	9 0	4 5

TT: Answers will vary.

Page 194
Estimates will vary. There are 12 pieces of candy.
TT: Answers will vary.

Page 195
Estimates will vary. Actual amounts include:
18 slices of pizza; no
20 hot dogs; yes
20 soft drinks; yes
hot dogs and soft drinks
pizza
two slices

Page 196
Estimates will vary.
There are 10 slices in each loaf; 20 slices in all.
There are 12 eggs in each carton; 24 eggs in all.
There are 26 pieces of popcorn in each pot; 52 pieces in all.

Page 197
There are 3 clowns riding.
2 more come.
There are 5 clowns in all.

Page 198

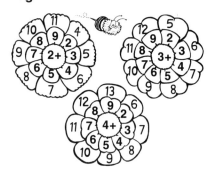

GB: 8 + 4 = 12. Rest of answer will vary.

Page 200
The total is 21.

Page 201
19 + 3 = 22; yes
12 + 3 = 15; no
11 + 6 = 17; no
23 + 8 = 31; yes
24 + 7 = 31; yes
18 + 12 = 30; yes
35 + 18 = 53; yes
TT: Answers will vary.

Page 202
GB:

58 + 25 83 PAID	22 + 12 34 WHO	12 + 13 25 DAY'S	30 + 17 47 GETS
12 + 17 29 JOB	37 + 15 52 NEVER	60 + 32 92 JANITOR	10 + 10 20 FULL
55 + 13 68 A	11 + 10 21 FOR	43 + 18 61 NIGHT	35 + 24 59 THE

Who never gets paid
34   52   47   83
for a full day's job ?
21   68   20   25   29
a night janitor
68   61   92

Page 206
165 + 158 = 323
yes
yes

Page 207
Path A is the shortest path.

Page 208

371 + 243 = 614
621 + 383 = 1004
963 + 174 = 1137
GB: 635 + 367 = 1002
1002 + 779 = 1781

Page 209

Page 210

21 triangles
31 cookies
76, yes
804

Page 211

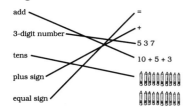

Page 212

Page 214

9 − 3 = 6
7 − 6 = 1
5 − 2 = 3
TT: Answers will vary.

Page 216

10 pinwheels; 5 less = 5
Think: 10 − 5
8 balls; 6 less = 2
Think: 8 − 6
6 kites; 4 less = 2
Think: 6 − 4

Page 217

GB: There are 5 trucks.
5 less than 9 = 4 vehicles left.

Page 218

Answers will vary.

Page 219

3 apples
14 pumpkins
11 doves
GB: Answers will vary.

Page 221

281 − 193 = 88
486 − 287 = 199
621 − 383 = 238
963 − 174 = 789
610 − 599 = 11
GB: There are 365 days in a year.
There are 366 days in a leap year.
There are 730 days in two regular years.
There are 731 days in one regular year and one leap year.

Page 222

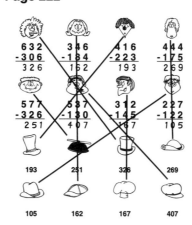

TT: Answers will vary.

Page 223

2 bears
20 pennies
3
138, yes

Page 224

There are 8 more s
than ⬭ s.

Page 225

GB:

Page 229

3 x 0 = 0
1 x 3 = 3
3 sails
GB: The number of problems solved in 30 seconds will vary.

6 x 0 = 0	3 x 1 = 3	2 x 0 = 0
1 x 1 = 1	5 x 0 = 0	4 x 0 = 0
7 x 1 = 7	6 x 1 = 6	3 x 0 = 0
2 x 1 = 2	1 x 0 = 0	5 x 1 = 5
4 x 1 = 4	7 x 0 = 0	

Page 230

1 x 1 = 1	2 x 4 = 8	3 x 5 = 15
1 x 3 = 3	2 x 6 = 12	4 x 3 = 12
2 x 0 = 0	3 x 2 = 6	4 x 4 = 16
5 x 2 = 10	6 x 1 = 6	7 x 3 = 21
5 x 5 = 25	6 x 3 = 18	7 x 4 = 28
5 x 6 = 30	6 x 5 = 30	7 x 6 = 42
8 x 3 = 24	9 x 2 = 18	10 x 0 = 0
8 x 6 = 48	9 x 4 = 36	10 x 2 = 20
8 x 8 = 64	9 x 6 = 54	10 x 4 = 40

Page 231

factors: 4, 2
4 x 2 = 8 fish altogether
factors: 5, 2
5 x 2 = 10 cookies altogether

Answers

Page 232

9 x 3 = 27

3 x 4 = 12

2 x 2 = 4

5 x 4 = 20

4 x 4 = 16

1 x 4 = 4

GB: Answers will vary.

Page 233

10 points x 3 tests = 30 points

4 bunnies x 2 carrots = 8 carrots

5 bears x 2 skates = 10 skates

Page 234

4 x 2 = 8 bananas

9 x 6 = 54 apples

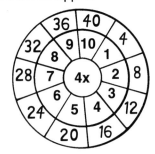

6 x 1 = 6

7 x 0 = 0

8 x 1 = 8

9 x 0 = 0

10 x 1 = 10

Page 235

6 trees x 4 leaves = 24 leaves altogether

Page 236

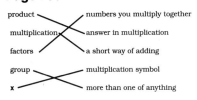

Page 238

1/3, 1/2, 1/2, 1/3

GB: *Parent:* Make sure child's drawings represent specified fractions.

Page 239

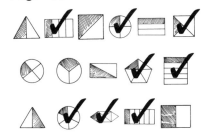

Page 240

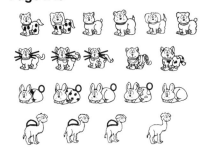

Page 241

1/5 is shaded; A

2/3 dogs have spots; C

1/2 milk is gone; D

2/4 pieces are gone; B

Page 242

Page 243

I AM TERRIFIC
5 12 6   10 3 8 8 5 4 5 2

AT   MATH!
12 10   6 12 10 1

Page 248

Circle frogs numbered 2, 4, 6, 8, 10, 12, 14, 16, 18, and 20. These frogs should be colored brown. All other frogs should be colored green.

TT: Counting by twos is faster.

Page 249

Circled items will vary. ***Parent:*** Make sure child draws 4 circles, each containing 5 toys. Counting: 5, 10, 15, 20.

GB: 10 can go into space.

Page 250

	A	B	C	D	E	F
Row 1		▨		▨		
Row 2		▨		▨		
Row 3		▨	▨	▨	▨	
Row 4				▨		
Row 5				▨		

Page 251

10, 25, 20, 85, 109

GB: 7, 14, 21

Page 252

Some answers will vary. ***Parent:*** Make sure child draws line to the correct number of digits in his or her answer.

365 days in a year, a 3-digit number; 10 toes, a 2-digit number; 8 spider legs, a 1-digit number.

Page 253

111, 379, 980, and 203 are 3-digit numbers; yellow

10, 12, 99, and 50 are 2-digit numbers; blue

3, 8, 1, and 7 are 1-digit numbers; red

Flag is horizontally striped from top to bottom: yellow, blue, red.

GB: Colombia, South America, Bogotá

Page 254

7 in the tens' place: 71, 73; blue
3 in the tens' place: 37, 39, white
9 in the tens' place: 96, 95; red
Flag is vertically striped from left to right: blue, white, red.
GB: France, Europe, Paris
Sample answers: the United States, Australia, and Chile also have red, white, and blue in their flag.

Page 255

10 clouds: the 1 is orange, the 0 is yellow
12 trees: the 1 is orange, the 2 is yellow
13 butterflies: the 1 is orange, the 3 is yellow
20 ants: the 2 is orange, the 0 is yellow

Page 256

10 monkeys: the 1 is yellow, the 0 is green
16 parrots: the 1 is yellow, the 6 is green
11 opossums: the first 1 is yellow, the second 1 is green

Page 257

7 in the hundreds' place: 726, 735; green
5 in the tens' place: 357, 352, 951, 450; yellow
3 in the ones' place: 243, 573; black

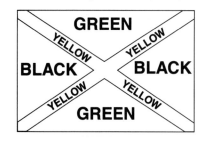

GB: Jamaica, Kingston

Page 258

Estimate: will vary
Actual: 53 leaves

Page 259

Estimate: stars in the sky, grains of sand, bubbles in soda are circled in green
Count: days in a week, kids in math class, cars in toy box, planets in solar system, buttons on telephone have purple squares around them
TT: Astronomers take a square section of the sky and count the stars in that section. Then they multiply that number by the number of sections they think cover the sky. Astronomers estimate.

Page 260

23, estimate, 900, 346

Pages 262–263

5 + 2 = 7
2 + 1 = 3
5 + 1 = 6
TT: l + 6 upside down becomes 9 + l, which equals 10.

Page 264

cherry has 6 letters, **tree** has 4 letters; 6 + 4 = 10; sample words are **watermelon**, **rhinoceros**
flower has 6 letters, **acrobat** has 7 letters; 6 + 7 = 13; sample words are **concentration**, **skateboarding**
GB: The pizza (5 letters = $5) and hamburger (9 letters = $9) would cost $14 altogether. You would have $12 ($4 + $8) and would not have enough to buy both. You would need $2 more.

Page 265

0 + 3 + 6 + 8 = 17

Page 266

Page 267

Fastest route: Calabasas to Bodega to Timbuktu: 23 + 14 = 37 miles

Page 268

Draw a solid line to connect 20, 13, and 6; the sum is 39.

Page 269

77	7	81	33	53	15
+16	+4	+12	+8	+17	+27
93	11	93	41	70	42
M	U	M	B	L	E

Answer: A MUMBLE BEE

Page 270

$153 + $251 = $404
They can buy the television, which is $400.

Page 271

200 + 1 + 50 + 100 + 150 + 50 = $551
Yes, Evan has enough for a new drum set, with $1 left over.

Page 272

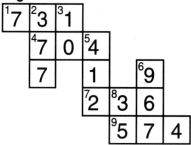

Answers

Pages 274–275
Ferris wheel, girl in car, hamburger stand

Page 276

9	4	8	7
−2	−1	−3	−6
7	3	5	1
M	A	T	H

Page 277
A = 8, B = 4, C = 7, D = 5, E = 3, F = 6

Page 278
5 − 3 = 2, 51 − 27 = 24; green
55 − 26 = 29, 29 − 2 = 27; yellow
98 − 30 = 68, 61 − 9 = 52; black
80 − 41 = 39, 50 − 20 = 30; yellow
98 − 11 = 87, 79 − 2 = 77; blue

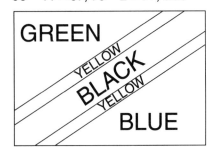

GREEN
YELLOW
BLACK
YELLOW
BLUE

GB: Tanzania, Africa, Dodoma

Page 279
14 people are on the train.
14 − 6 = 8; 8 people are left.
8 − 1 = 7; 7 people are left.
Yes, he will have enough people.

Pages 280–281
Colin can buy the sled. He will have $29 left.
Trevor can buy the in-line skates. He will have $15 left.
Dylan can buy the walkie-talkie. He will have $1 left.

Page 282

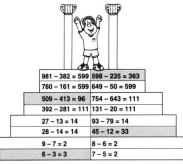

981 − 382 = 599	598 − 235 = 363
760 − 161 = 599	649 − 50 = 599
509 − 413 = 96	754 − 643 = 111
392 − 281 = 111	131 − 20 = 111
27 − 13 = 14	93 − 79 = 14
28 − 14 = 14	45 − 12 = 33
9 − 7 = 2	8 − 6 = 2
6 − 3 = 3	7 − 5 = 2

TT: Answers will vary.

Page 284

7	7	8	5	8
×7	×5	×9	×7	×7
49	35	72	35	56
S	E	V	E	N

10	8	5
×10	×2	×7
100	16	35
A	T	E

7	9	8	7
×8	×9	×7	×5
56	81	56	35
N	I	N	E

Answer: Because . . . SEVEN ATE ("8") NINE

Page 285
2 × 2 = 4 cups of flour
1 × 2 = 2 cups of cocoa
3 × 2 = 6 eggs
1 × 2 = 2 sticks of butter

Pages 286–287
5 × 2 = 10
GB: *Parent:* Make sure child colors fingers 1, 3, 5, 7, and 9 green, and fingers 2, 4, 6, 8, and 10 blue.

Page 288
①×⑤=△5 jet engines
②×⑤=△10 wings
⑩×⑤=△50 tires

Page 289
5 × 9 = 45; black
7 × 8 = 56; red
6 × 4 = 24; orange
Flag is horizontally striped from top to bottom: black, red, orange.
GB: Germany, Europe, Berlin; sample answers: France, Italy, Spain, Austria

Page 290
1. 3 × 4 = 12   2. 7 × 9 = 63
3. 6 × 3 = 18   4. 7 × 8 = 56
5. 6 × 7 = 42   6. 9 × 9 = 81
7. 5 × 5 = 25   8. 10 × 3 = 30

START	12	16	64	89	40
24	63	32	12	18	21
90	18	56	42	81	25
76	20	40	77	24	30
15	63	55	37	18	FINISH

Page 292

1/2	1/3	1/6	1/2	1/3
1/6	1/4	1/2	1/3	1/6
1/2	1/3	1/4	1/6	1/4
1/4	1/5	1/2	1/3	1/6

1/2 = one-half
1/3 = one-third
1/4 = one-fourth
1/5 = one-fifth
1/6 = one-sixth

Page 293

1/5   1/3
1/4   1/6

Page 294

¼   ⅕   ⅓   ⅙

GB: 1/2, or one-half, of the Earth is lit by the Sun and 1/2 is in darkness all the time. The lit side is called **day** and the dark side is called **night**.

Pages 296–297

Game winners will vary.

$4 \times 9 = 36$
101
$27 + 23 = 50$
$467 - 234 = 233$
$33 + 44 = 77$
$147 + 218 = 365$
25
$100 - 18 = 82$

Page 298

39	88	42
−11	−27	−40
28	61	2
W	I	N

7	5	6	8	7
×8	×6	×9	×5	×7
56	30	54	40	49
P	L	A	C	E

59	33	61	67
+12	+45	+59	+62
71	78	120	129
S	H	O	W

Answer: WIN, PLACE, SHOW

Page 299

4 hands × 3 fingers on each hand
= 12 fingers
12 fingers (Amos) − 10 fingers
(you) = 2 more fingers
3 feet + 3 feet = 6 shoes; or 3 feet
× 2 brothers = 6 shoes
2 antennae (Amos) − 0 antennae
(you) = 2 more antennae
GB: $3 \times 6 = 18$ footprints

Page 300

$3 \times 6 = 18$
$20 - 3 = 17$
$3 \times 7 = 21$
$200 - 150 = 50$
$346 + 79 = 425$
GB: More than one math symbol fits because the **sum** of $2 + 2$ and the **product** of 2×2 are the same. The answer for both is 4.

Page 301

$126 + 321 = 447$
$97 - 66 = 31$
$3 \times 5 = 15$
$27 - 18 = 9$
371

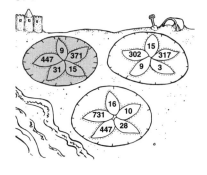

Page 302

GB: 25 spokes × 2 wheels = 50 spokes; or 25 spokes + 25 spokes = 50 spokes